THE MEDIEVAL TOWN

THE
MEDIEVAL
TOWN

❀

FRITZ RÖRIG

University of California Press
Berkeley, Los Angeles, London
1971

University of California Press
Berkeley and Los Angeles, California

First published 1967

© Propylaen Verlag, 1967

Library of Congress Catalog Card Number : 67-26961

Third Impression, 1971
ISBN: 0-520-01088-4   *(Cloth)*
0-520-01579-7   *(Paper)*

FOREWORD

Fritz Rörig occupied the Chair of History at, successively, Lübeck, Kiel and Berlin, becoming an Emeritus Professor at Berlin in 1950. He was a member of the Berlin Academy of Sciences, until his death in 1952.

The essence of *The Medieval Town* first appeared in volume IV of the Propyläen *World History* (edited by W. Goetz) in 1932. The complete version, which was prepared from the original manuscript by A. v. Brandt and W. Koppe, was first published in 1955.

An English translation of this classical exposé has long been overdue. For this edition a full and entirely new, annotated bibliography has been prepared by Dr D. J. A. Matthew, Reader in History at the University of Durham.

CONTENTS

Contents

Contents

THE ILLUSTRATIONS

The Illustrations

ACKNOWLEDGMENT

The Publishers wish to thank the following for permission to reproduce illustrations included in this book:

Albertina Museum, Vienna, for fig. 21
Alte Pinakothek, Munich, for fig. 25
Bayerisches Nationalmuseum, Munich, for figs. 13 and 22
The Belgian State Tourist Office, for figs. 12 and 35
Bibliothèque Nationale, Paris, for figs. 9 and 31
Bibliothèque Royale, Brussels, for figs. 8 and 30
Bildarchiv Foto Marburg, for fig. 14
The Trustees of the British Museum for figs. 1, 5, 20, 28, 29 and 33
The German Information Bureau, London, for fig. 36
Pierre Jahan, Ypres, for fig. 15
The Landesmuseen, Brunswick, for fig. 26
The Mansell Collection, for figs. 16, 18 and 38
The Radio Times Hulton Picture Library, for figs. 7 and 11
Staatliche Museen, Berlin, for fig. 24
Süddeutscher Verlag, Munich, for figs. 4, 25 and 26
Verlag Ullstein, Berlin, for figs. 3, 6, 29 and 37

1

THE RISE OF
A NEW POWER

❀

After the end of the eleventh century when the knights of Romance-Germanic Europe joined forces in the concept of a united Christian West, it seemed as though the crusades were to be the highest expression of the ecclesiastical and knightly civilisation of the time. But the way in which the movement developed and ended was to compromise both the concept and those who had subscribed to it. Its great and lasting consequences are not those which had originally been intended; they were engineered by people who saw how to exploit the movement to their own entirely different ends. At the very time when the crusading movement was getting under way on a large scale, an element of political activity was already in existence in the towns of northern Italy—a factor which, having first proved its strength in the fight for independence against the established local seigneurial powers, now set about employing its newly-won freedom of activity in the service of the economic and political expansion of the town. For these towns the crusading movement was in point of fact a splendid opportunity for putting their commercial instincts into practice. Their intervention changed the whole face of Mediterranean trade; furthermore it laid the foundations for the unprecedented rise of these towns during the centuries in which the crusades took place, which otherwise would have been impossible on such a scale.

As far as political independence and economic strength were

concerned, none of the Italian towns was better equipped than Venice for tackling the new tasks that emerged in the world as it was around 1100. Certainly Genoa and Pisa had also risen to full autonomy by this time, and achieved a well-earned reputation as maritime powers; but Venice far outstripped them on both counts, and had the advantage of longer-standing relations with the Levant in which the former were only just beginning to take an interest. Although Venice had outgrown its dependence on the Byzantine sphere of influence, the links that connected the Adriatic and Byzantium were by no means severed. Constantinople was the largest and, in the fullest sense of the word, the most progressive town on the Mediterranean, in which ever since antiquity the life of a big city had been maintained and developed to an incomparably greater degree than, for instance, in Rome. But Venice's relations with Constantinople did not consist merely of isolated commercial links; it was rather a question of a spiritual affinity, which even in the tenth and eleventh centuries gave the city of lagoons a strange kind of ascendancy within the western world. Moreover the sea-power of Venice was indispensable to the Byzantine Empire, ever since the establishment of the Normans in southern Italy about 1080 had threatened her position of power. It was the Venetians' policy to make capital out of this military weakness in the advancement of their trade within the Byzantine sphere of power; for their help in defeating Robert Guiscard in 1084 Venice had already been rewarded with freedom of trade throughout the whole Greek Empire. But even before this the concession of buildings and properties suitable for trade in Byzantium itself had been one of Venice's most coveted rewards.

This pattern would certainly have made itself felt when the crusaders and soon afterwards the crusading countries had to approach the Italian towns for naval assistance; this assistance was provided but only of course against substantial reward for the services rendered. More important than a share of the booty were the gifts of whole living-quarters in the most important harbours of the Syrian coast. In the first years of the great crusades Genoa made particular progress in this direction; Pisa was soon left behind. In the long run it was Venice which gained most from the new system of establishing bases in harbours in the Levant. Her lead over her Italian rivals was too great. It was founded more than anything else on the Venetians' trading establishments in Constantinople itself. The Greeks regarded with increasing resentment Venice's position in the commercial life of Constantinople as an unbearable usurpation on the part of the hated Latins. They gave vent to this hatred in violent measure, without, however, succeeding in breaking the Venetians' ascendancy in the Byzantine empire; the Greek empire offered too many positions that could easily be taken by the Venetians with their maritime supremacy, and this gave the Venetians a welcome opportunity for entrenching themselves in all kinds of places. This meant, for Venice's position on the distant Syrian coast and in the crusading countries, an excellent protection for her flank and her intermediate bases which her Italian competitors had to do without. Venice had firm bases all along the Syrian coast; similarly she was clever and unscrupulous enough to secure her southern flank by means of direct negotiations with the Islamic powers themselves, the Sultan of Egypt among others. Without doubt the Venetians also made a profit out of furnishing the Saracens directly and indirectly with war supplies. There was no power in the West that could have stopped them doing this—only papal prohibitions had the slightest effect. The culmination of these egotistical realist politics within the crusades themselves was the transformation of the fourth crusade (in the first decade of the thirteenth century) organised by Venice itself, into a fairly large-scale conquering expedition designed to further the ends of the commercial republic of Venice. Never was the Venetians' domination of the political leadership of the crusading bands stronger; never was their policy of exploitation more openly visible than at the plundering of Constantinople in 1204.

It must have been a particularly forceful kind of energy that proved strong enough to transmute the crusade movement—the strongest expression of applied medieval faith—into its own complete antithesis. Nor was this energy solely of a political nature; behind Venetian politics there stood one dominating force—the desire for economic expansion and supremacy. Trade was at that time the branch of economy which alone could lay the foundations

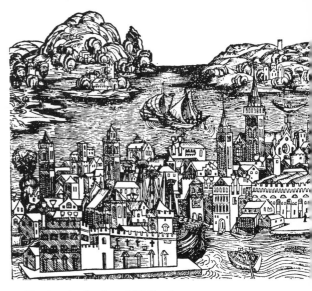

1   Venice, in the late Middle Ages

of dominion over widespread areas. Obviously not a kind of trade
run by shopkeepers and pedlars, but one that lay in the hands of
the economically strongest and socially most distinguished inhabitants of these towns whose names were spoken with the
highest admiration even by contemporaries. This was particularly
true of Venice itself. At one time certainly the topmost stratum of
the town's society had been formed by those who possessed estates
on the Italian mainland—but such people could maintain their
influence and increase their wealth only if they were prepared to
suffuse their whole thinking and aspirations with the demonic
urge for the increase of wealth and power, for, with the inclusion
of the Italian towns in the economic heritage of Moslem trade,
this urge was achieving its unprecedented successes in medieval
Europe. In Venice too those *homines novi* who made their fortune
by trade alone were finding their way to political power and social
distinction. A class of long-distance and wholesale merchants was
the driving force behind the eastern policies of the Italian towns.
But there was an even more profound causal relationship be-

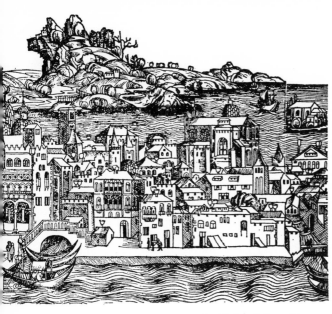

From Schedel, 'Weltchronik', 1493

tween towns and trade. It is certainly true that the towns of northern Europe grew up under the shadow of seigneurial powers.
Whether it was a question of the resurgence of a town amid the
ruins of a decayed Roman town on the Rhine or the Danube, or of
the first beginnings in the ninth or tenth centuries of a town life in
the Germany Rome had never known, the bishop as landlord, and
subsequently lord of the town, determined the life of the urban
settlement that was growing up. Economically, in that his ecclesiastical entourage (which was supported by rich manorial properties), for a still modest urban settlement, formed indispensable
consumer groups whose constant needs made a daily market
profitable and, indeed, possible. Legally, in that subsequently the
new urban settlement areas were given, by royal charter, special
municipal privileges favouring the episcopal authorities and not
the town corporation. But the situation did not last long in which
the only opponents of the lord of the town were a group of more
or less dependent workers. The urban settlements, which to begin
with, and up to the last half of the tenth century, were of very

modest proportions, attracted a new group of residents—long-distance traders, who brought their own law with them. Also, they had a strong feeling of solidarity which they had developed on long combined trading journeys which at the time were still conducted in the cooperative manner of a caravan. Nor did the traders who settled in the new towns wish to abandon this spirit even when they were at home. The guilds were the inevitable consequence. This was where they met together, this was where they celebrated their festivals, which occasions were liable to be rather more sumptuous than the spirit of ecclesiastical decorum considered appropriate, and quite different from what was familiar and understandable to ecclesiastical and monastic thinking. In the guilds people cultivated common interests, even when they threatened to come into conflict with the sphere of economic and political power of the episcopal authorities. Thus the guild of respected merchants became of itself an organ in which the whole urban population had an interest. In the eleventh and even the early twelfth centuries, the more the episcopal lord of the town forced the whole population, particularly the artisans, to even greater efforts and productivity in all directions, by means of his power of excommunication within the town, the clearer it became that the merchants' guild was an organisation in which the small man in the town—the artisan and the small shopkeeper—saw a remedy for his complaints against the bishop and his officials.

But there was another side to the coin. The upper class of merchants, whether organised in guilds or not, was already in the eleventh century and far more so in the twelfth clearly in economic ascendancy over the artisans, and the latter were dependent on it. Even then it was self-evident that the merchant upper class was the owner of the most valuable urban property. In those towns in which the most recent critical research has examined the conditions in detail—for example Paris, London, Cologne, Regensburg, Dortmund, Münster, Soest, Goslar and Wroclaw—it has established the extremely significant economic, social and legal contrast between the property-owning burghers with interests in long-distance trade and the mass of artisans living mainly on property they did not own. It was a serious matter for the artisan in Cologne for example that he had to offer his wares for sale, and even produce them, in market stalls, covered markets and bakeries belonging to members of the upper class of long-distance traders. It was the same for those who plied a trade; they went about their business in workshops and mills belonging to the same people. Nothing could be more mistaken than to assume that in the German, French and English towns of the eleventh or twelfth centuries there was any kind of economic or social equality. The inequality was not even confined to the fact that in the old episcopal towns there were knights and servants of the bishop himself. This sector of the population, which to begin with and even in the eleventh century—as in Worms and Cologne—could be relied upon entirely to support the lord of the town, became in the twelfth century more and more identified with the interests of the long-distance traders and in the thirteenth it fused entirely with the upper class, and finally dissolved into it. There is no greater proof of the uncommon power of the foreign-trading upper-class burghers than the fact that it managed to absorb the knightly elements that had originally been on the bishop's side. The only other thing to compare with this is the fact that the trading class had managed to achieve a privileged position with regard to urban property. Not that property was a major consideration, for the revenue from it did not furnish even the possibility of any business worth mentioning. It may have happened that the original owners of rural and urban property became long-distance traders, but at least as common as this were the cases of trading families developing, so to speak, from nothing, into urban and also rural estate owners, as for example the Girs and the Overstolzens in Cologne. Such properties in any case, in the early centuries of the swift rise to power, only remained with families and individuals who were in active contact with trade, which at the time was swiftly creating new values of its own. The function of these properties within the structure of their owners' economy was to act as an insurance against setbacks in trade.

Thus the rise and fall of the individual's position in the general distribution of property was determined by his successes or failures in trade. In the Middle Ages, of course, long-distance trade and property belonging to the urban *bourgeoisie* went hand in hand;

but what determined this connection, and what made it necessary, was trade. Undeniably, in the hands of later generations rich properties offered an incentive to live off the income; to give up working as a businessman and spend one's life in respectable idleness; but the early centuries of the rise of the town, swiftly creating as they did new and greater ideas of value, were simply not favourable to the idea of being content to live off unearned income. Even within the landed upper class one individual's property might go back originally to feudal times, having belonged perhaps to the former official property of the lord of the town, and another's might have been acquired through foreign trade. And though the one might be so engrossed in a life of gain that the zealous friar would have occasion to rebuke him for being possessed by the devil of acquisitiveness, and the other might exhibit features of a more lethargic, more comfortable nature, believing in the joys of a *jeunesse dorée*: nevertheless, despite the apparent inner heterogeneity of the class, it enjoyed as a whole an uncommon degree of uniformity, and was seen by the lord of the town on the one hand and on the other by the lesser folk of the town, particularly the artisans, as a powerful force, the active leading class of the town and of the burghers' efforts towards self-betterment. The fact that its members were continually changing, that individuals on the way down disappeared from its ranks, and that, conversely, the financially successful found easy access to it until the fourteenth century, only served to increase the energy of this leading class.

It was almost a matter of course that these fundamental changes in the distribution of economic goods, the rise of a class that in the opinion of the time was unusually well off within the population of the town, should also be expressed in a redistribution of political power. The man who most immediately sensed the strong urge for power in the new class was the man who formerly wielded the political power—the lord of the town. In the most important towns on West German soil it was the bishops, whose dominion over the populations had been expressly confirmed and extended in the tenth century by the Ottonian imperial and episcopal policy. Up to the eleventh and even the twelfth centuries it still looked as if the power of the bishop, relentlessly extending its competence over the town, was making progress and would eventually transform the entire urban population into a passive object of the lord's will to dominate. Strasbourg, Worms and Speyer felt this perhaps most acutely; even more so the smaller episcopal towns such as Besançon. Out of the confrontation between a burgher upper class becoming conscious of its economic strength, and a lord of the town striving towards the permanent subjection of this class a heavy tension developed. Out of the conflagration of large-scale politics jumped the spark that caused this situation of tension to explode. When in 1073 the Rhenish bishops turned against Henry IV, the Bishop of Worms discovered for the first time that his dominion over the town was by no means absolute, and especially so at the moment when he turned against the very authority from which he had received, signed and sealed, his power as lord of the town—the monarch. After his defection from the king, the townspeople were not to be disposed of as though they were a horde of serfs without wills of their own. The unexpected happened: the bishop who had defected from the king was driven out of the town by his townspeople, and the king, who had been in the greatest danger, welcomed into the town with all honours. What first manifested itself in Worms on German soil—the desire of the urban population to be independent of seigneurial authority—became from then on an extremely important factor of political life. If, as in Flanders, the lord came half-way to meet this desire, he gained the most positive support for his own power; it was not until 1128 that the Flemish towns decided against accepting the French king's candidate for the throne who was relying on the nobility for support. As a rule however, things were different, especially with the lords who were bishops. The proximity of the two parties in the restricted space of a town continually gave rise to new areas of friction.

Then began a long period of altercation between the lords and the burghers striving for autonomy which was not settled until the fourteenth century. This settlement, in most of the Rhenish towns, represented victory for the burgher movement for autonomy. This period of transition in the political life of the burghers contained scenes of drama and bloodshed. On the night of 2 May 1232 flames from the burning town hall lit up the grim faces of the burghers of Worms who, in an unfavourable phase of this eventful struggle, preferred to destroy with their own hands the symbol of their autonomy rather than have it destroyed by the bishop who at the time was in alliance with the king. In 1262 the people of Strasbourg fought for autonomy on the field of Hausbergen; in 1288 the famous battle of Worringen was fought in which the people of Cologne overcame the archbishop and his entourage with a coalition of his princely enemies. But although there was more than enough real bloodshed in this dispute between totalitarian and autonomous power, it is equally true that the power of the lord of the town was being weakened all over the place in the process of a slow development, frequently undetectable in detail, until finally it was undermined and retained at the most only the appearance of power in externals, if at all.

This upper class of the towns, long-distance traders by virtue of their commercial origins, as *cives majores*, or people of rank, led the way for the rest of the population and exercised on the lord's ministers who were entrusted with administrative tasks such a power of attraction that the latter became more and more identified with this class and less and less with their lord. It was the same class that from the beginning had been the driving force of the whole townspeoples' freedom movement, and which was also behind the brotherhoods, the *conjurationes* with which the burghers' emancipation in Italy, France and England—and also in Germany (Cologne)—had begun. Not without reason did Lambert von Hersfeld, who hated the urban movement, give vent to his wrath over the *praedivites*, the class of rich merchants which had led the Cologne rising of 1074. Real expertise in matters of urban economy, which at that moment was flourishing, and wealth in solid gold made it possible for this class to usurp more of the lord's sphere of power. Control of the market, of the provision trades, soon even supervision of all the trades, regulation of weights and measures, possession of the very valuable market buildings— all slipped out of the lord's hands into those of the townspeople, particularly those of the burgher upper class. The lord's right to mint coinage was very soon encroached upon; as early as 1174 the Archbishop of Cologne mortgaged all his minting rights. In the thirteenth century a large number of Rhenish bishops had to agree to a combined supervision of coinage through municipal organisations. In the fourteenth century, in towns such as Basle, Strasbourg and Erfurt, it became entirely the townspeople's province. Other towns such as Cologne itself, Worms, Speyer, Augsburg, Regensburg and Mainz only achieved this later on. A similar process brought about the burghers' encroachment on the lord's monopoly of tolls in which the traders had a particular interest. But the aspiring burghers made inroads even into that sector of the lord's sphere of activity which was not of such direct economic interest to them. The levy of direct taxes became the responsibility of the burgher authorities; above all, from the thirteenth century onwards the towns gathered individual taxes by means of the so-called *Ungeld*, brushing aside the lord of the town's protests about breaches of his monopoly of taxes.

Even the most obvious sovereign rights—military and judicial sovereignty—slipped slowly out of the lord's hands in the larger towns. The rising at Cologne for Henry IV in 1106 actually put the burghers in possession of the town's fortifications; 100 years later the town was the formal owner of the fortification rights after it had surrounded Cologne—in spite of many differences of opinion with the archbishop—with the huge surrounding wall of 1180. Mobilisation of the fighting strength of the local population and stiffening it with enlisted mercenaries was in the thirteenth century already an accepted right of the larger German towns; a clever man such as Bishop Henry of Basle was content enough to recognise the full, including the military, independence of the burghers, so long as they would not refuse him their help as an ally. Even the general legal sovereignty of the lord was in most cases infringed. The legal and judicial authority ceded to the burghers over the town market soon spread over the whole town, took hold of voluntary jurisdiction, particularly of the property laws, splendidly developed by the towns, and did not stop at criminal and even capital jurisdiction.

These specific changes in the episcopal towns of Old Germany did not occur simultaneously or with uniform regularity; it all depended on individual circumstances how opportunities presented themselves for encroaching on the lord's sphere of power. But in spite of individual variations in the process, its chronology and intensity were fundamentally the same everywhere; it represented the replacement of the seigneurial by the autonomous principle. Success for the burghers' movement was however only made really visible, externally, and permanently assured when the collective management of the town and of all the acquired rights was taken over by a centralised burghers' authority. This was the council, the government of the town by councillors, or *consules*, as they had first developed in the Italian towns. In the larger towns of northern Italy around 1100 government was by self-elected *consules*. This was the more remarkable in that before the Italian burghers' communes were formed a struggle took place between the well-represented nobility of the towns and the new, purely burgher upper class, until both amalgamated into a unified class composed of those who qualified by virtue of their property and those involved in long-distance commercial enterprises. It was this class that from the end of the twelfth century was in possession of the council. The council was here, as elsewhere in Europe, the organ of the upper class of burghers, and actually ruled over the rest of the population, even though it started out as an organ of the whole population and was seen as the latter's representative in opposition to the various old seigneurial powers within the towns. In those German towns in which the council emerged from the old leading class of nobility, as in Cologne or Soest, the introduction of a formal council system meant, as far as the inhabitants of the town were concerned, little more than the more exact definition of the constitutional forms in which the hitherto existing supremecy of the nobility operated. In the Rhenish episcopal towns the council did not appear until 100 years after it had in Italy; its position was still problematic up to the middle of the thirteenth century. While the councillors of the Rhenish towns were reaching out with a splendid policy of alliance—the league of Rhenish towns—into large-scale politics, they were at the same time strengthening their position *vis-à-vis* the previous lords of the town. From then on until far into the fourteenth century was the heyday of the aristocratic constitution of the councils in Germany; then new efforts were begun, which terminated in the lower classes of the town being given a share in its government. It has left behind two visible legacies: the one, the proud seals of municipal charters in the quiet seclusion of the archives, the oldest of which go back to the twelfth century and the most beautiful of which were cast in the thirteenth. They were the unequivocal sign that the town as cor-poration could act in its own right and thus bind itself legally by letter and seal. The other, which even today is the pride of many a town whose past has been significant, is the town hall, seat of autonomous government.

The changeover to autonomy had a very important consequence for the entire urban population, expressed in the legal maxim which illustrates the graphic nature of medieval legal language, 'Town air brings freedom'. The development of autonomy occurred simultaneously with the transition from the personal to the territorial principle in law. No longer were old relationships of a personal nature to decide the legal standing of the individual, but the judicial area of the place he was living in. With the pro-nouncedly seigneurial character which the area of urban juris-diction still bore around 1100, it looked as though the consequence of the territorial principle for the towns would be that everybody who came into the town automatically became the lord's serf. But this is only true of the very earliest indications of the way the territorial principle took effect in the towns. The seigneurial character of the territorial principle made itself felt in the country-side; here in many places the cry was, 'Air means possession', which reflected the fact that the village in the height of the Middle Ages was subject to a magistrate who ruled the whole village. It was quite different in the town. As far as uniformity in the legal position was concerned, in the sense of free and not free, com-petence was in the hands of the ruling class of the town and no-where else. But after 1100 the free status of the burgher upper class was no longer in doubt. It was on this account that the de-mand for general freedom of the urban population became an internal necessity. But on this account, too, the demand was heavily championed by the leading class on behalf of the entire popula-tion, particularly for the new arrivals, because it was necessary to eliminate legal claims deriving from relationships of dependence of individual inhabitants on outside lords, if the integrity of the urban jurisdiction was not to be endangered. It is not surprising, furthermore, that all the powers of the old feudal order in law and society should resist the towns' claim that the serf of a secular lord who came into the town should be a free burgher of the town after a year and a day; nevertheless the new legal principle was established. Indeed the towns for their part engaged in an offensive against the country lords when they accepted aliens, who were under the dominion of some lord, as burghers of the town. These were called 'citizens of the pale', that is to say, 'those who lived in the suburbs of the town'. Until far into the Middle Ages the towns were able to maintain this challenging institution. But the legal uniformity and freedom of the urban population remained. This was one achievement of the urban movement, and laid the foundations for all subsequent periods. The idea of personal bondage disappeared within the walls of the towns; the innumerable relationships of dependence in the countryside—in short, the feudal ordering of society—were broken and subdued. This was the burghers' doing, and it laid the basis for their subsequent designation of the proper relationship of the individual to his state as 'citizen of the state, not a subject'.

Nevertheless, this development must not be allowed to obscure the fact that equality before the law was by no means matched by economic and social equality. Relationships of dependence through debts or financial commitments could be more oppressive than political bondage or semi-bondage had been; even in the constitutional life of the town small trace could at first be seen of equality. Any progress in the enlargement of the burghers' sphere of power still went in favour of the nobility; everywhere the lower classes were complaining of exploitation by the *potentes*. On top of this, distinguished burghers frequently employed smaller townspeople, particularly artisans, in the form of *muntmannen*, as a very dubious bodyguard. In 1258 the archbishops of Cologne complained about provocative occurrences of this kind. During the fighting among the nobility which allowed Regensburg no peace at the beginning of the 1430's, the leaders of the warring families kept forty or more such *muntmannen* about them with whom they walked about the streets stirring up trouble. In the Italian towns the fighting between the factions of individual families took on far more drastic forms.

2   Florence in the fifteenth century
From a contemporary woodcut

PUSHING EASTWARDS

❁

The German towns we have dealt with up to now have been those on Old German soil, and particularly the Rhenish episcopal towns. But there can hardly be a more convincing proof of the colossal strength these burghers possessed than the energy, method and circumspection with which as early as the twelfth century, although they had still by no means obtained satisfaction in their political demands, they undertook an enormous programme of colonisation. This was the time of the great movement of population that led the Germans across the Saale and the Elbe into those regions, thinly populated with Slavs, that had been abandoned by Germanic tribes in the centuries of the mass migration. One of the peculiarities of these eastern territories on which Berlin, Wroclaw, Leipzig, Dresden, Gdansk and Kaliningrad now stand was that urban life was almost completely unknown to them. It is an honourable page in the annals of the Old German towns that they were capable of making unprecedentedly large-scale use of the position they had acquired by opening up the eastern territories. For it is due to them that urban settlements grew up in the eastern lands from the middle of the twelfth century onwards, based on the mature example of the Old German towns, though simplified in a practical way and therefore superior to them. Without doubt they founded these settlements in agreement with the political powers of the new lands—German princes like Henry the Lion, or even

Slavonic princes who were well disposed towards the German immigrants. Many a sovereign privilege bears witness to this goodwill. But to regard these privileges, and thus the princes who granted them, as the actual supporters and organisers of the urban settlements of the twelfth century would be to misunderstand the nature of medieval privileges and indeed the relationship between ordinance and real life.

As early as 1120 the Duke of Zähringen had allied himself with twenty-four distinguished merchants in a *coniuratio* to found Freiburg im Breisgau, a notable achievement of urban colonisation on Old German soil directly before the great eastern colonisation began. In the hands of these twenty-four merchants lay the actual execution of the town's foundation; into their hands flowed the profits of the risky work, and from the start they took on official functions. From the start therefore the new foundation was endowed with a ruling class of burghers which by virtue of its commercial reputation, its privileged position in urban property and its superiority in the constitutional life of the town, dominated the mass of the population. This was a faithful reflection of the sharp social distinctions that existed within the places of origin of the Freiburg upper class, among which Cologne particularly should be mentioned. A little before this the original town of Brunswick was founded by burgher enterprise, as was also presumably medieval Vienna, on the site of an almost completely abandoned Roman camp. The motive force behind the foundation of Vienna was however that the long-distance traders of Regensburg wanted to have a secure intermediate base on their expeditions to far-off Kiev. It is easy to see here how the foundation of new towns was connected with the important lines of commerce. In this case the actual founders were the Regensburg traders; their protectors the margraves of the eastern territories.

The significance of great commercial connections for the birth of urban settlements is even more clearly seen in the Baltic region. The chronological and geographical sequence of their coming into being points to a close correlation with the lines of commercial traffic. From Lübeck, which emerged in its final form in 1159, to the Swedish island of Gotland stretched the line along which the towns were first founded. It was here that in the twelfth century the town of Wisby came into being, where ruins today speak mutely of a former greatness—a German foundation whose population was at first predominantly German. The line of urban foundations continued over to the other end of the Baltic, on whose coast Riga and Reval sprang up; and, pushing farther into the interior, Dorpat. From Lübeck via Wisby to the Baltic stretched the domains of various lords; for this reason alone the initiative of individual princes cannot be the essential cause of the process as a whole. But from Lübeck the way led via Gotland and the Baltic coast to Novgorod on Lake Ilmen with its wealth of furs; this was the magnetic pole of attraction. Thus the whole thing begins to take on significance. Bold entrepreneurs from the Old German towns, from Cologne and Soest, Dortmund and Münster, but also from Bardowiek, the oldest trading place in the lower Elbe region, undertook the risky business of founding towns on a grand scale, made Lübeck into a strong base and thus made themselves independent of Schleswig, the former point of departure for Baltic traffic, which at that time was not German. Here, too, we have the absolute supremacy of the long-distance trading syndicate in the division of property, in economy and in the system of government right from the start. The fully developed urban settlement, wholly concerned with trade, represented, along with the cog (a ship which, since it had a larger hold, was superior to the Scandinavian galley for regular trips) the most important means by which the older Scandinavian and Slavonic traders in the Baltic region could be beaten in peaceful competition. It must have been a very important event for the German merchants when the great urban emplacement of Wisby on Gotland proved a success—on Gotland, the strongest and most flourishing seat of the old masters of the Baltic, the Scandinavian peasant-merchants. It was here that the superiority of the urban settlement over the rural as a stronghold of trade was most clearly demonstrated; it was a struggle for the peasant-merchant to realise, as he finally did, the hopeless nature of his position and to move into the new and new-fashioned town of Wisby. For the German merchant from the lower Rhine to Novgorod, however, Wisby became the seat of the ʻassociation of mer-

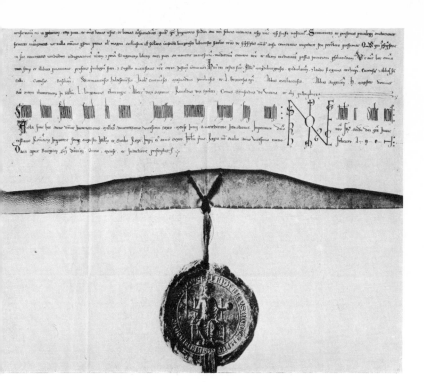

3 Charter of the City of Lübeck, 1226: bottom portion of charter and seal

4 Cologne in the fifteenth century
Detail from 'The Martyrdom of St Ursula'

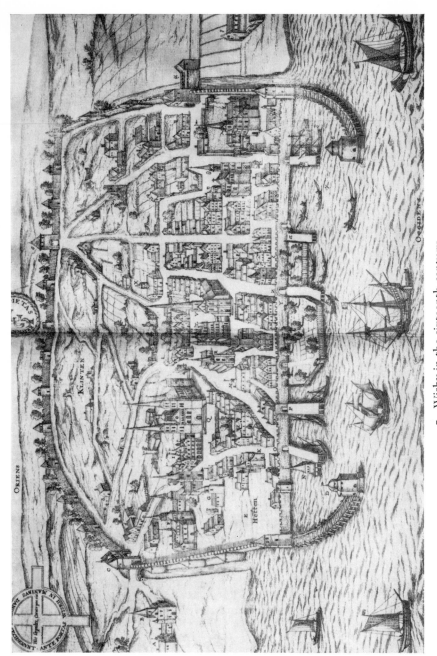

5   Wisby in the sixteenth century

chants of the Roman Empire who visit Gotland'. The systematic founding of towns that started out from the Rhineland and West-phalia thus created in the Baltic zone an important network of new towns which, with the common origins of their inhabitants and close economic bonds between themselves, furnished the solid foundation of the subsequent Hanseatic League.

If in the Baltic region it was trade that dictated the direction in which towns sprang up, mining also exercised a similar function. Freiberg in Saxony, the mining towns of Bohemia and Hungary may be mentioned in this connection. In any case—the most important new towns of the twelfth and also of the early thirteenth centuries were created in the main by enterprising burghers of the Old German towns; not until the thirteenth century were in-numerable agricultural towns founded by local lords, which frequently were of no commercial importance.

Those new towns which sprang from the burghers' initiative provided at the same time the best ground for a swift and easy development of urban government. They had no episcopal master with whom they had first of all to wrestle for power. On the contrary, the burgher entrepreneurs who organised the foundation of these towns provided not only the upper class from which councillors could be drawn but also, to all appearances, with their original organisation frequently numbering twelve or twenty-four, the basis of the council itself. Without conflicts, almost un-noticed, councils were formed in towns such as Freiberg and Lübeck around 1200; in point of fact it was simply a question here of the transference of the imported Italian title of *consules* to the burghers' council that was already in existence. The frequently repeated fact that newly colonised territory moves faster in questions of political organisation than the mother country, with her burdensome remnants of older forms of organisation, holds good for the history of the German town. Because of this the con-solidation of sovereign rights in the hands of the council was achieved much more quickly in the new towns. Sufficient to say here that even before 1225 the Lübeck council had the right to inspect the mint at any time, and in 1226 the town obtained full rights to strike coinage; this occurred far earlier than in other

German towns, particularly the older episcopal towns of which Trier (Trèves), Bamberg and Würzburg never succeeded in obtaining the right.

This attempt to grasp the profounder significance of the urban foundations in the Baltic area ended of its own accord with the visible beginnings of the greatest German alliance of towns, the Hansa. At the peak of its history we can postulate the odd-sounding thesis that the whole existed before the parts. For the very origin of these Hanseatic Baltic towns, among them the proud town of Lübeck, subsequently their leader, was not a matter of chance but was carried out according to a conscious economic and political programme: the commercial supremacy of the German merchant in the Baltic. This creative idea came into being in the towns of West Germany. The manner of its execution, the pushing forward of bold groups of entrepreneurs from one urban foundation to the next, brought about an alliance of the leading classes which was not only an economic one but also—which goes a long way to explain the subsequent league—a blood relationship. And as the lesser people of the same region followed their leaders there resulted, as the shift of population went on, a community of origin amongst the lower classes as well, which was effectively encouraged by the exclusion of people of Slavonic origin from the guilds. Just as in documents Latin gave way to the vernacular, the language written and spoken in Riga and Lübeck, in Wisby and the Hanseatic settlement in Bruges was an identical form of Low German. An economic community created by the planning and activity of blood relations—such was the community of Germans on the coast to which the merchants from West German towns belonged as much as did those from Riga or Dorpat; thus it was with the subsequent Hansa. One can say that around 1300 those who were weaving the meshes of the political net in Münster or Cologne in the west, in Lübeck, Wismar or Stralsund in the south-west corner of the Baltic, and finally in Riga or Dorpat on its eastern shores, were members of the same families. It was with profound significance that Reval wrote to Lübeck in 1274: 'The two towns belong together like the arms of Christ crucified.'

What the German merchants had achieved and created from the

middle of the twelfth century until well into the thirteenth was a position of monopoly in Baltic trade; with the proclamation of free competition (to which anyone who feels himself to be economically the stronger is always glad to subscribe) Scandinavian and Slavonic traders were almost completely cut out. On the basis of their supremacy in the traffic in eastern products, which were indispensable to western Europe, the Hanseatic merchants made themselves supreme in Bruges, the largest reloading point in Western Europe. From Novgorod to Bruges the German merchants had created a new, highly organised trading system; they had united northern Europe for the first time in an important economic entity. An entity composed, certainly, of strongly differentiated elements—in the west: the highly developed industrial area; in the east: the colonised territories of Europe as they were then, the north-west of Russia with its superabundance of raw materials. But it was precisely in this variety that lay the exceptionally high profit potential for the merchants who controlled the supplies of goods, in other words the Hanseatic merchants. The main line of east–west traffic was successfully completed by a north–south connection. Lüneburg, on whose salt production the whole of Northwest Europe was dependent, sent its products to Lübeck from around 1400 on the Stecknitz canal, the first German inland canal of major importance, which connected Lübeck with the Elbe near Lauenburg. From Lübeck two important routes branched down to South Germany, to Frankfurt am Main, Strasbourg and Nuremberg, and from there across to the Mediterranean region, mainly to Venice. A much-prized traffic in Icelandic hunting-falcons went on between Lübeck and the Sicilian court of Frederick II, going via Nuremberg and Venice, and even as far as Alexandria. Furs and amber from the Prussian coast found their way down to the Mediterranean. A lively north–south trade developed in Norwegian dried cod and herrings from Scania, both commodities on which the Hanseatic merchant had laid a firm hand. Both kinds of fish went as far as northern Italy, as German commodities; there was as much trade in Hanseatic herring in Prague as there was in Vienna, Regensburg, Nuremberg or Salzburg. With its production of dried cod Norway bought corn and flour from the Hansa. In the west–east trade Flemish and later also English cloth preponderated over everything else; in competition with eastern furs, corn and other bulk goods, particularly Swedish copper and iron, were pushed more and more out of the picture.

In the thirteenth century the organisation of the subsequent Hanseatic trade still lay not in the hands of a league of towns but with the Gotland Association. But the same century saw the home towns of the German merchants who visited Gotland coming more to the forefront. From among them Lübeck won its position as leader in its fight with the most geographically dangerous competitor that the Hanseatic economic system had to contend with on its most vulnerable side. This was Denmark, which either threatened or controlled the land connection between Lübeck and Hamburg and the sea connection between the Baltic and the North Sea, the Sound and the Belt. At the beginning of the thirteenth century Lübeck had even had to acquiesce to Danish protection as the lesser of two evils. However as soon as it was at all viable Lübeck energetically attempted to shake off the Danish control; this happened in 1225. In 1227 she took a glorious part in the final ousting of Danish control in Holstein. It was thanks to this typical mixture of diplomatic skill, this great farsightedness and readiness to make the ultimate sacrifice at the right moment, which was to be found in the political leadership of Lübeck at the time, that the threat of Danish imperialism in the broad Baltic region as far as Reval was eliminated. At this time the founder of the Teutonic Order, Hermann von Salza, the Germans in Livonia and the council of Lübeck were in close alliance. The Emperor encouraged their common undertaking from Italy by raising Lübeck to the status of an imperial city in 1226, thus giving it the formal foundations for its subsequent autonomous life and putting it in a position to remain a base for operations for German colonisation in Prussia and Livonia and yet to continue independent of Denmark, without which everything would have remained in danger. As Lübeck fulfilled, beyond all expectations, the hopes that were cherished in those critical years in the broad Baltic region, the town gradually came to practise an autonomous Baltic policy independent even of the Gotland Association. The policies of the Lübeck council were implemented with resolution and assurance throughout the following decades. Their most important method was a very skilful policy of alliances into which, they were even able to bring the princes, by making use of their mutual disagreements. Establishment of peace on the land and sea routes was, together with peace locally, the first concern of the alliance, although it was not long before others followed. The treaty signed by Lübeck and Hamburg in 1241 dealing with their combined resistance to highway robbers between the estuaries of the Elbe and the Trave already provided for mutual measures which applied to the internal relationship of the towns. The first currency alliance between two towns, Lübeck and Hamburg, followed in 1255. As early as 1265 the towns near Lübeck agreed to come together annually to carry on their common business. In 1280, Lübeck and Wisby signed a treaty to promote peace in the Baltic, which Riga joined in 1282. All this no longer had anything to do with any really decisive executive power vested in the old Gotland Association; in fact at that time the power in the Baltic region already lay in the hands of the towns flocking round their leader, Lübeck. To begin with, though, the semblance of power was left to the venerable association in Gotland, as for example when in 1292 it again authorised a trade deputation to Novgorod. But the authorised deputation consisted of burghers of the three towns of the Baltic alliance—Lübeck, Wisby and Riga. Only a few years later in 1298, when the Westphalian towns in their turn sent their representatives to Lübeck, this deference was no longer considered necessary. Lübeck was authorised to negotiate with Novgorod, and further use of the old seal of the merchant association of Gotland was expressly forbidden. The Gotland Association no longer existed; the era of politics controlled by the allied towns from Gampen to Dorpat under the leadership of Lübeck had begun.

Thus the German Hanseatic League of Towns already existed in its essence, even though the name as such only appears in 1358. However, a new Danish advance to the south at the beginning of the fourteenth century, which Lübeck had to accommodate, made everything uncertain once more. Only the death of the Danish king, Eric Menved, removed from Lübeck the threat of

permanent Danish supremacy. The old leadership had to be
laboriously won back again. And when about the middle of the
fourteenth century the alliance of the towns of the Hanseatic
League had gained under the leadership of Lübeck a stronger
power and organisation, everything was imperilled yet again by a
new imperialist wave from the north on the part of the Danish
King Waldemar III. This time it was decided to offer military
resistance. Evidently both the diplomatic and military leadership
fell to Lübeck. When this failed to bring victory, Lübeck put
its commander-in-chief and mayor Johann Wittenborg to death.
Only thus did the council think it could restore its reputation with
the allies and its authority *vis-à-vis* its own population. Only success appeared to justify enjoyment of the respect that membership
of the council brought with it; whosoever failed to achieve it was
sacrificed by the association in order to save the dignity of the institution. In the second war against Waldemar, which took place
mainly in 1368, Bruno Warendorp, a second Mayor of Lübeck lost
his life; this time as a glorious general of the allied towns which had
come together in the Confederation of Cologne of 1367. It was of
great significance that the highest military success granted to the
Hansa was won in the struggle against Denmark, a country that
was fateful for the league. The peace of Stralsund of 24 May 1370
represents the highest achievement of Hanseatic and Lübeck
policies. A great thing had been achieved, something that excited
the amazement and admiration of the contemporary world:
Denmark, by its geographical position the most dangerous opponent of the German towns, had been vanquished. The surrender
of the Sound fortifications to the allied towns for a period of fifteen
years was the clearest expression of the military and political
victory; the security and extension of trade privileges, that of the
economic victory. Acquisition and defence of foreign privileges was
after all the *raison d'être* of the Hanseatic League, which had no
desire to be a constitutional federation and only waged wars in
special alliances as circumstances demanded. These trading privileges in all the northern countries, in England and Flanders—
privileges which sometimes even put the German merchant
abroad in a better position than his colleague at home—were the

prize that the German merchant sought after with his monopoly in the Baltic. Northern Europe and parts of Western Europe were dependent on him and on his supplies. No wonder that he laid claim to the reward for these provisions. This reward was determined by the privileges of the countries dependent on his supplies.

It is impossible to understand the existence of the Hanseatic League if one only looks at the external progress of this remarkable movement. The Gotland Association, a body capable of political action whose decisions were valid and had authority as far afield as Bruges, represented an older form of commercial life, which is as difficult for us to understand as the Gotland Association itself. This was itinerant trading. In boats, or caravans called *hanse*, the merchants went out together, frequently travelling astonishingly great distances. Around 1100 it could happen that the same Regensburg merchant visited Kiev in the east and Cologne in the west. A North German merchant from Soest, for example, had to brave the long road to Novgorod and, with the wares he had purchased there, continue as far as England or Bruges if he wanted to extract the greatest gain from his eastern wares and take back to the east the goods that were most sought after there. The point of this kind of trading was to fetch a quantity of goods, even though it might be relatively small, from its place of origin, and bring it to the place where it was most sought after. The longer the journey the greater the profit—this was the motto. The very boldness of these journeys should ensure that modern appraisal does not lower the early medieval itinerant tradesman to the status of a hawker just because the itinerant tradesman of our time now exists only as such. But there were times, even into the thirteenth century, in which all trade was itinerant trade, even the socially respectable long-distance trade that handled larger quantities of goods. This primitive stage of commerce was characterised by the exchange of goods in various buying places, with the trader himself accompanying the goods. Over sea and shore went the merchant, as the picturesque language of the time describes it. That form of external organisation of the communal interests of German merchants offered by the Gotland Association thoroughly suited their needs. For the island of Gotland was indeed the place where such groups of travel-

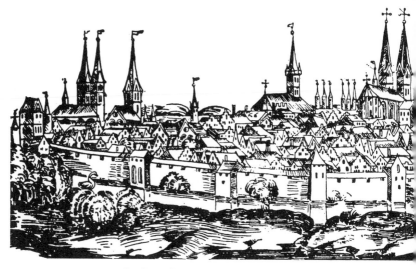

6 Lübeck in the late fifteenth century

ling merchants continually met, especially during the most important seasons of the year for trade journeys. But in the thirteenth
century the old conditions changed. It was not just that advances
in navigation had made Gotland less indispensable as a base; more
significantly, the age of the older kind of itinerant merchant was
now over. If we were to put a northern German merchant of around
1300 next to one of around 1200—between these dates lies a period
of transition—we would find an antithesis of the greatest significance: the merchant has become sedentary. His business methods
are quite different. The business no longer travels around with the
merchant and his merchandise. It became a solid establishment—
the *skrive-kamere*, as the business-rooms of the Lübeck merchant
Johann Wittenborg around 1350 were appropriately named. For
it is here that we find the profounder reason for this change. In
the thirteenth century the merchant adopted the use of writing or,
more particularly began, towards the end of the century, to make
a quite different use of writing. It then became an accepted fact
that the more distinguished merchants of a leading trade centre

From Schedel, 'Weltchronik', 1493

could do business with writing, reading and written accounts and know Latin—though not perhaps the classical style of Cicero.

Important as this in itself must have been for trade, still more important was the variety of uses the merchant knew how to make of his encroachment on a field of learning hitherto restricted to the church. With the help of the small, unpretentious sheets of parchment he used for his letters, the merchant could now manage the various establishments within his sphere of activity from a firm central point, simultaneously for example in Novgorod and Bruges. Sealed documents, even bills of exchange, that were legally binding on the merchant, were sent out; the answering documents and letters came back from his business correspondents and went into the merchant's coffer, in whose false bottom a stock of cash in local and foreign currency was to be found. Long-term payments were agreed before the town notary in the presence of the foreign business associates and were entered in public credit books; trading books, of which the individual merchant kept several, served as a basis for checking outstanding payments and

facilitating settlements between relations and companies. The commission business came to be extremely important in the Hanseatic
economic area; it allowed the merchant to stay at home and at the
same time to sell his goods in various places. Young people from
the office travelled on the head's business to foreign trading places,
in whose commercial houses they had learned their business
in early years, and their zeal was fortified by the subsidiary
transactions of peaceable business made with their boss. Business
associates in foreign places served as representatives there; goods
could be sent regularly without personal convoy through
the freight and removal business, particularly the then highly
developed shipping companies. This did not mean that the merchant no longer travelled. Important business reasons such as the
purchase of a particularly large quantity of goods or participation
in a foreign fair such as Frankfurt meant that the head of the house
had to travel just as much as he does today. But at that time the
business no longer travelled with the merchant; it was carried on
at home, perhaps by a relative who then settled up when the
owner came back. It is one such arrangement that we have to thank
for the oldest Hanseatic merchant's notebook that we possess,
which was personally kept by the brothers-in-law Hermann
Warendorp and Johann Klingenberg, who were connected with
families on the Lübeck council, at the beginning of the 1340's. Both
brothers-in-law had their own businesses, and were not even in
any business relationship. But when one of them was out of Lübeck
the other represented him in the winding up of certain transactions.

From these activities we get a clear picture of the state of the
business at the time. Johann Klingenberg was commissioned by
one Ludolf de Monte to sell 120 tons of corn on his account in
Lübeck. The corn came into Lübeck on various ships. When it
came Johann Klingenberg was away. Whereupon his brother-in-
law Hermann Warendorp immediately took his place. To the last
farthing he entered what he had to spend on freight, unloading,
winnowing the corn and brokerage, and what he had got back by
selling off a part of the corn while his brother-in-law was away.
Conversely Johann Klingenberg, when his brother-in-law was on
a business trip to Flanders, looked after the sale of a large quantity

of cloth, in which once again the commission system was employed as a means of trade. The Warendorp–Klingenberg notebook gives us an insight into a commercial concern of average importance; the accounts show that there were far more important merchants in Lübeck at the time. It was no rarity for a firm to be concerned with wholesale trade in cloth and at the same time to go in for particular kinds of Flemish cloth; nor that it should resell Flemish cloth in Lübeck in parcels of up to a hundred pieces. The total import of Flemish cloth to Lübeck in 1368, which was almost entirely in the hands of the Lübeck merchants, can partly be calculated exactly and partly reliably estimated. It amounted to about 23,000 pieces, which nowadays would be worth several million pounds. These 23,000 pieces of Flemish cloth, which in the unsettled times of 1368 reached Lübeck via Oldesloe, can well bear comparison with the 16,000 pieces of cloth which, according to the Doge Tommaso Mocenigo, the Florentines supplied every year for export to Venice. In the best years of the Florentine cloth manufacture—the middle of the fourteenth century—it certainly produced three to four times more than the Lübeck cloth importation. In another direction too the Lübeck cloth trade of around 1350 proved itself structurally more advanced, and nearer to the Italians, than has been supposed: its traders were no longer small drapers who were also involved in retail, but pure wholesalers who bought cloth in bulk and sold it in bulk.

The growth of a large group of sedentary wholesalers such as could be seen in Lübeck around 1300 dealing in Swedish metals, Lüneburg salt, corn and furs as well as cloth, represented one of the most noteworthy results of the inner change that had taken place in the Hanseatic merchants—the rationalisation of trade by the use of the written records which they had learned to make use of as a factor in organisation. No longer did the merchant's strength lie in travelling around with his colleagues, but in the degree of organisation in his own concern. Thus purely individualistic characteristics emerged which had distinct effects of a social nature going beyond the sphere of commerce. At the end of the thirteenth century Lübeck, as a result of the organisational advances made by its merchants, went through a period of the greatest economic prosperity. Between 1280 and the beginning of the fourteenth century the rate of interest for money invested in stocks dropped from ten to five per cent—a clear indication of the increase of capital seeking investment. Fortunes were continually being amassed purely by trading activities to such a degree that old ideas of fortune and wealth were abandoned. The unfortunate results of this splendid boom had however to be borne by those who had been satisfied with their wealth and had not participated in the commercial boom. What only a few years previously had been riches became in relation to the newly amassed fortunes a modest affluence. Income which came mainly from investments would not go far enough to keep up the standard of living; and so *rentiers* began to touch their capital. So long as one had property, it was easy enough to find money-lenders among the new style of merchants. But if one could not pay the interest the creditor mercilessly took possession of the security: transference of property into new hands was the result. Into the possession of the new men fell the beautiful stone corner houses of the old founder-families, their warehouses on the Trave, their stables that served as collecting houses for agrarian produce, and all the buildings that, because of the rising rents paid by the artisans who were dependent on them, were particularly sought after—market stalls, bath houses and bakeries.

There were real family tragedies in Lübeck at the end of the thirteenth century. Obviously at such a time there was no shortage of people who made their living from lending money. But how dangerous such businesses were is demonstrated by the example of the Lübeck councillor Hermann Clendenst, whose career as a banker was brought to an end, as was his associates', in 1335 by a crushing bankruptcy. The kind of people who made up the council provide a clear picture of the social regrouping: the strong parvenu found his way on to the council while the tired men of the waning economic star disappeared from it. Thus the council was at the disposal of the strongest, most powerful men. Their policy took effect with the suppression of the Gotland Association; they were now able to throw their influence into the balance far more strongly from Lübeck. Their policy, with all its hardness and ruthlessness, formed the relationship between Lübeck and the

Hansa and Norway. This country which in the second half of the thirteenth century was way behind Lübeck in economy, technology and commercial experience very soon ended up in a situation of dependence which one can only call Hanseatic domination. Dried cod and butter, the most important Norwegian exports, were monopolised by the Hanseatic merchants. A true spirit of enterprise, or if you like, a capitalistic spirit celebrated its triumph with the integration of Norway into the Hanseatic economic zone; but it left behind it the discontent that the economically weaker, rightly or wrongly, bears towards the exploiter.

However, since this same policy did not operate solely in the private economic field but also summoned up the courage and self-sacrifice necessary to political activity on a grand scale, it achieved the greatest possible success—victory over the Danish threat and the peace of Stralsund of 1370.

7   Seal of the Hansa merchants at Novgorod

3

CITY AND STATE

❧

The Hanseatic towns' war with Waldemar of Denmark was obviously waged to defend not only the internal political autonomy that the German towns had achieved but also complete international freedom of trade. The question immediately arises of the relationship between the authority of the state and the development of the towns, a relationship that differed widely in individual European countries. To begin with Germany, the confrontation between the authority of the state and urban autonomy had in no way played itself out in the struggle (that we have already touched upon) between towns and their lords who had only come to power in Ottonian times as supporters of the authority of the king. The burghers' striving for autonomy of necessity had a considerable influence upon the relationship of the towns, the king and the state. The first time that the conflict between the towns and their lords flared up in Henry IV's reign already indicated the community of interests shared by the burghers and the monarchy in this dispute. In the years that followed, this community of interests emerged more and more clearly: the towns offered the king the possibility of dealing directly with the mass of his subjects, and winning over the towns as trustworthy supporters of the royal power. Conversely, for the towns, a strong monarchy was the surest protection against excessive demands on the part of the lord, against despotic attempts by the princes to divide up the kingdom, and thus also the economic area of the towns' long-distance trade, with customs barriers; and later on against the threat of being swallowed up and subjugated by the gradually forming territories. But at the time when all these burning questions required settlement by a single German authority, the monarchy, the central power of Germany, was already weakened to the core and no longer free in its decisions.

This is not the place to show how the glittering splendour of the idea of the imperial crown, stemming as it did from the ideas of the late classical period, had weakened the German monarchy and prevented it from solving these highly important internal questions which had been put to it in exactly the same way as they had to the French or English monarchy. But this fact must certainly be recognised as most important for the understanding of urban development in Germany in the Middle Ages. Since 1125, when the princes' right of free voting was proclaimed, this German monarchy had no longer any real freedom of action. It was dependent on the princes, whose interests it had to consider on account of its Italian policy. It was not that later kings failed to recognise the importance of a royal policy towards the towns. But only in the rarest cases were they sufficiently independent of the princes to risk embarking on such a policy, which logically had to be one directed against the princely lords of the towns. It is a saddening spectacle to see how even a man of the greatness of Frederick II launched time after time a royal policy towards the towns only to be obliged to give it up out of respect for the princes and his Italian policy. When his son Henry, as his representative in Germany, was careless enough to defy the bishops in a number of episcopal towns in favour of the burghers, Frederick himself had to quash, in Ravenna in 1231, all the autonomous constitutional organisations which had sprung up in the German towns without episcopal agreement—a measure which in point of fact was effective only in Worms, where the bishop had put it into operation. The movement was too powerful to be suppressed by decrees. For the crown it was a heavy blow to its authority; for the towns, to begin with, nothing more than a disappointment. In spite of this they went their own way, since their own strength was sufficient to carry on their contest with the power of the lords. They also remained well aware of their community of interests with the monarchy: in the troubled times of the interregnum the alliance of Rhenish towns was quite a large and initially successful attempt to use the political strength of the towns to guarantee an undisputed election of a king, to protect the kingdom during the interregnum and maintain the energetic pursuit of peace in the land.

However, after the monarchy had renounced its independent influence on the urban movement, any further development of the relationship, in the sense of a rigid subjection to the king, between the monarchy and the towns which had achieved autonomy by their own efforts, was out of the question. The urban units of government in the late Middle Ages stood politically in relation to the king in the same way as did the units of power represented by individual princes and lords. Only they were of far greater importance to the king as sources of income. The 'imperial cities', as later the former royal towns were called, insofar as they had not been lost by the notorious method of mortgaging themselves to other lords, paid their fixed annual amounts, of which an index of dues of 1241 gives more exact information; over and above this they raised, along with the episcopal towns which had achieved autonomy, additional taxes for the king amounting to very considerable sums, and in particular bore the expenses of parliament and the court. The towns generally gave their money willingly to the state; but one thing they demanded—recognition of their autonomy in that the individual town should pay its dues as a whole, and that its internal tax system should not be interfered with. When Rudolf of Hapsburg attempted at the beginning of his reign to encroach upon the towns' taxation system and to tax the individual burghers directly, there was serious and even military opposition. Rudolf was clever enough to give in, for which the towns were subsequently prepared to meet even greater demands.

The relationship between the towns and the king after the interregnum was more of an alliance than a real political subordination. This was most clearly expressed when the towns rallied to the king's support in the event of a projected war, as for example the crushing of the Rhenish Electors' uprising in 1301. Municipal circles remained convinced of the necessity of a close relationship with the king. As late as 1344 in the Frankfurt convention of towns the

8   A Commune receiving its charter
From Bibliothèque Royale, Brussels, MS. 9242, f. 274

9   Philip the Fair and his Council in 1322
From Bibliothèque Nationale, Paris, MS. français 18437, f. 2

prophetic statement was made that the towns stood or fell with the state. Lewis of Bavaria, the last German king who had to fight out the frightful conflict between secular and spiritual power, again found in the towns his most faithful support. A late testimony of this leaning towards king and empire, already in an age of entirely different ideas, and thus the more touching, was given by Strasbourg in the famous document presented to Charles V in 1552, in which it asked the emperor for his help against the French, who were threatening the town, after an attempt at a surprise attack had been bravely beaten off. By his help, the document continued, the emperor would 'protect this town from final destruction and make it into a strong bulwark for the whole of the river Rhine', and would also 'thus highly delight the whole of the river Rhine'. Then follows, clearly stamped with thoughts of alliance which even here lay at the bottom of it all, 'We for our part would be eager to lay down our lives and property in the protection and saving of this town, and to save and keep the same to the utmost of our ability within your Majesty's Holy Empire'. Even at this late stage the leaning towards the empire still existed with such a high degree of clarity and farsightedness; towards an empire, unfortunately, that no longer had the slightest interest in such things.

Only by virtue of this league-like form of relationship between imperial cities—at the end of the Middle Ages about sixty or seventy of them, mostly in the south—and the king and empire does their political activity within and without the boundaries of the empire become understandable. From about 1250 up to the end of the fourteenth century the right of towns to form alliances amongst themselves and with other princes was self-evident and expressly recognised by the king, as, for example, by Albrecht in 1301—provided that the law and the honour of the king and empire were respected. The Golden Bull of 1356 permitted alliances of towns, though, only insofar as they were implemented within the framework of the public peace alliances and included the local princes concerned. It was not this imperial regulation, however, that put an end to the great town alliances of the Upper Rhine, but the defeat of these towns by the princes at Döffingen (1388). Whether and how far alliances between towns were still possible was determined, from the end of the fourteenth century, by the actual power relationships between towns and princes.

In most of the other German territories too the relationship of the towns to local princely power, to the 'lords of the land', had the character of an alliance until well into the fifteenth century. Rural sovereignty was still neither geographically nor structurally an exclusive, undivided right which would not tolerate any other constitutional organisation. Of real territorial states there were as yet very few; rather each of these lords exercised a number of individual rights. This was the position with the relationship between the lord of the land and 'his towns'. In many cases the lord's rights were confined to his receiving homage as supreme lord; the towns even forbade the lord to build a fortified home within his town, as for example Wismar did with the Mecklenburg princes in 1300 and afterwards. Even when in 1311 Wismar was defeated in armed conflict with the lord of the land, who was supported by the princes of Lower Saxony, its right of alliance with other towns was not questioned; in the period that followed the town made energetic use of it. It remained one of the most faithful members of the Hansa. As late as 1581 the town declared that it would be reduced to poverty were it to be excluded from the Hansa for just one year.

The policies of their towns in alliance frequently had highly undesirable consequences for the lords of the land, as when Rostock in 1485, in energetic implementation of a decree of the allied towns, took an official of the lord and his servant and executed them out of hand as beach robbers because they had attempted to exercise the rights of wreck claimed by the lord as part of his old legal position. Now at last the coastal towns were able to assert their independence of their lord; they were so much lords of the sea themselves that in the sixteenth century the burghers of Wismar and Rostock could prohibit their lord from using their harbours for his own ships. And their mastery of the sea assured them a far higher degree of mutual military assistance than the German towns inland were able to muster amongst themselves.

Things were different where the territorial power had consolidated unusually early, as in Austria. Vienna lost its indentity as an imperial city as early as the thirteenth century. The town was subjected to an unusually intensive seigneurial rule; there were no alliances among the Austrian towns and no associations. The Austrian land lord in the middle of the fourteenth century was already, with a remarkably early display of absolutist measures, taking vigorous action in purely municipal matters such as the question of the redemptions on property holdings. But Austria was the exception. Even in such a rigidly organised territory, by medieval standards, as the German state, the towns took a stand against rural sovereignty both as members of an alliance amongst themselves and as a whole in alliance with the Hansa. What was possible in the way of real independence on the part of the 'princes' towns' of North Germany is best shown by the extremely cleverly and energetically run politics of Lüneburg. In the struggle between the Welfs and Saxons over the succession to Brunswick-Lüneburg, Lüneburg decided the issue for decades. In 1392 it brought the estates of the duchy together in an alliance against the lord, who had to buy the financial assistance he needed from Lüneburg by fully renouncing his power to rule in favour of a corporation strongly influenced by Lüneburg. The whole of Hanseatic policy would be incomprehensible without the looseness of the relations between the towns and their various lords; only three—Lübeck, Goslar and Dortmund—were imperial towns subject only to the king, although in 1388 Dortmund was obliged to defend itself against an unsuccessful attempt by a coalition of princes to overpower the town and deprive it of its imperial character. Around 1400 a new and fundamentally different era began in the relationship between town and state in Germany, in which the state was no longer represented by the empire, but by states which were shutting themselves off and pressing for a closed, centralised power vested in the lords of the land.

Up to this point, of the development of other European towns, developments in Italy had the greatest similarity with those of Germany, at least in the nature of their relationship to larger political organisations. As the Italian towns were responsible for achieving their own autonomy, they also fought for imperial recognition of their autonomy and their right to form alliances as early as the twelfth century. This was the well-known struggle with Frederick I, who finally recognised their municipal sovereignty over the urban territory and granted them free election of their consuls, and, above all, allowed them the right to form alliances amongst themselves. This was the essential and lasting result of the peace of Constance in 1183. For the things that Frederick I demanded in return were forgotten in the catastrophe in imperial Italian policy that occurred with the death of Henry VI. Even Frederick II's attempt to bring the Italian towns under a centralised and absolutist system by means of an extremely comprehensive act of organisation perished with its author. It is a fact of profound significance that both those countries which provided an immediate stage for the universal policies of the Emperor—Germany and Italy—suffered in the formation of their national state and ended in extreme political disunion and internal strife. But in the territorial formation of states on the old imperial soil in Italy the towns had a far more important role to play than they did in Germany. In Germany the political future belonged to the emergent states bearing the stamp of territorial feudalism. The formation of territories by the imperial towns did not produce zones of power of any significant size, even in their greatest manifestations, as for example the territory of Nuremberg; and the country towns, until the fifteenth century, were only able to assert their independence when the circumstances were favourable. Not so in Italy. Here the towns did not develop, as in Germany, within the power system of the countryside, but grew at the expense of feudal power areas until finally city-state bordered on city-state. The rural nobility was forced into the municipal sphere of interests. But in the process the leading classes of the individual towns—with the sole exception of Venice—lost their internal solidarity. In all the larger towns families of different political outlook—even the old opposition of Guelphs and Ghibellines was still going strong —regarded each other with hate or mistrust; at the same time the lower classes, organised into guilds, were striving for political power. The basis of the old council was destroyed, that is, an upper class so settled within itself that it had been able to allot consulships among its members without too much trouble. The conflicts between the patrician families were precisely over the consulship.

The country renowned for having won for Europe the constitutional government of towns by a council, confined it, around 1200, to alien governors (*podestas*). Only an alien of good standing, who was not entangled in the local family feuds, seemed to provide a guarantee that public safety and order, but above all peace in the town, were protected. It was he who administered justice, and frequently exercised military command. It was a highly paid, temporary office that demanded close supervision and frequent changes. The same people took on the governorship of various towns one after the other; frequently there immediately ensued exchanges between individual towns. The office was a profitable but also a dangerous one. Many a noble family knew how to put its members in such positions in various places. When not even the governorship was enough to bring peace to the towns, a new form of government developed, frequently out of the governorship— the Signoria. This became the political form under which the Italian city-states enjoyed their greatest splendour and also terrible troubles and convulsions; it was one of the great political and social prerequisites of the Renaissance. The result of the quite peculiar development of the Italian towns was this: the towns, having achieved autonomy, dominated the whole country, but because of the warring elements in their leading class and the pushing forward of the lower class, lost their opportunity of keeping the aristocratic form of government working ; as a result they sought and found salvation from strife in the absolute authority of individuals. But however much the later internal constitution of the Italian towns may have differed from that of German towns, Germany and Italy were the only countries in Europe, between 1250 and 1400, to be identical on one essential count. Only in these two countries did the towns enjoy a sufficient degree of freedom from larger political units to permit of their having an independent foreign policy.

The problem of city and state was resolved in a quite different way in those countries that had remained uninfluenced by the fateful consequences of the struggle between imperial and papal universalism—most importantly France and England—at least as far as the formation of their internal political relations was concerned.

Around 1200, at the time when in Germany the misfortune of
Henry VI's sudden death was taking its effect, in France the monarchy began to revive. Its most important internal political measure was the building up of an adequate bureaucracy that was
thoroughly effective and implicitly loyal to the king—a measure
of great importance which the German emperors had only attempted to carry out in Sicily. Its opponents were the feudal powers,
finally overcome more thoroughly by the quiet, centuries-long
work of the royal officials than by the clash of arms. In the struggle
with feudalism the towns identified themselves with the king
through their community of interests. Those towns which had prevailed over their lords sought support from the king, but looked
about them for guarantees of their independence; these were the
villes libres. The king confirmed with his privileges the legal position they had achieved by their own efforts thus subjecting them, at
first almost unnoticed, to a supreme royal sovereignty. More and
more these towns depended on the king to protect the constitutional position they had obtained—towns which had certainly
attained various degrees of communal self-government, but in
whose government the feudal princes themselves played a considerable part, exercising functions of a financial, judicial and military nature, and even influencing the nomination of the first
official of the town, the mayor. This position was occupied by the
king himself in the towns of his immediate sphere of power, and
particularly in the most important, Paris. From the twelfth century
onwards the merchants' guild in Paris, the association of *marchands
de l'eau* also known as the Parisian Hansa, emerged unequivocally
as the leader of the communal movement. It is easy to see how in
Paris these long-distance trader's guilds, jealously guarding their
monopolies in Seine trade, became the mouthpiece of the towns'
desires for self-government, and how the private, privileged corporation was transformed into a public authority. But this did not
mean that the rights enjoyed by this self-government were any less
restricted than they had been; the head of the local government of
Paris was still the *Prévôt Royal.* Still, in the time of Philip Augustus
II two rich burghers farmed the office of *Prévôt Royal* and thus provided the distinguished burghers with a real share in the royal

10 Assembly of the Provostship of the Merchants of Paris
From a woodcut of 1528

government of the town. But even at Paris, by the middle of the century this important office became one which was filled directly; from then on the *Prévôt Royal* was no more than a royal official.

Philip Augustus II was certainly a true friend of the French *bourgeoisie*. There were internal reasons for the connection. The royal system of government with its well-paid officials stood much closer to the bourgeois world than to the feudal one which it was to supersede. The king was quite prepared to meet any economic demands, as the *Marchands de l'eau* of Paris often found out. He also called upon the *bourgeoisie* to carry out state duties on a grand scale, by giving it a share in the general governmental duties of the country. During his absence in the Holy Land, the royal treasure and indeed the royal seal were entrusted to six burghers of Paris. In every town representatives of the *bourgeoisie* stood side by side with the royal officials. Philip knew very well how to use the outlook of the townsmen for the formation of a unified national idea of government. On the other hand the king, who was working towards a quite different stability of the national structure, was reluctant to surrender any of his rights in the form of privileges to individual towns. It would in any case have been senseless to diminish the old sphere of feudal rights and bring them under royal domination, and at the same time allow urban autonomy to mature into full independence; in exactly the same way, conversely, that in Germany it was impossible for Rudolf of Hapsburg to interfere with urban autonomy and at the same time to recognise the independence of the lords and princes. It therefore meant an adjustment of the relationship of city and state, which was striven for and achieved under Philip, when, in the consolidation of his dominion over Toulouse, the consulate was replaced by a college of *Prud'hommes*, nominated by the royal government. The consular constitution of the towns of southern France, which here too were in the hands of single rich families, was already at the beginning of the thirteenth century evidently no longer really capable of survival, for the same reasons as in the Italian towns. This is clearly indicated by the fact that a whole series of southern French towns that were still outside the direct sphere of power of the king (Nice, Arles

Marseille, Avignon and Tarascon) went over to the *podesta* system, drawing alien *podestas* from Italy.

From the time of Philip Augustus it was settled that in the France of the French kings there would be no room for a full freedom of the towns after the manner of Italy or even Germany. What Philip Augustus had begun his successors systematically continued. As the power of the crown trespassed upon the jurisdiction of the towns with consular constitutions in the south, and that of the *villes libres* or communes in the north, so urban independence moved towards its end. The sharp contrast between the rich families that held the consulships and the lesser folk gave the monarchy a skilfully used opportunity to play off the lower strata against the upper; already the fact that several of these towns could themselves see a solution of their internal troubles only in the *podesta* shows that they were ripe for a successful intervention by an alien authority. French towns of the twelfth century comprised a far more varied series of individual types, particularly with regard to their municipal constitution, than the German towns. Superficially the heterogeneity may have remained; but in fact it disappeared under the strong grip of centralising monarchy. Under Philip the Fair the political subordination of the towns to royal power and its official apparatus was as good as carried out, which did not exclude the possibility of towns keeping their self-government in certain fields —finance, law courts, police—though even here intervention by national bodies on account of actual or alleged mismanagement was always possible.

In these circumstances it was of great importance to the French towns what kind of man was ruling this state to which they were subject. For the townsman and the merchant, even with their limited independence, life was good under a man like Louis IX (1226–70) who was honoured both at home and abroad as the 'personification of Justice'. National affairs under Philip the Fair (1285–1314) opened up possibilities for unprecedented advancement for those of the bourgeoisie who had acquired a legal and literary education. Guillaume de Nogaret, the king's awe-inspiring adviser, who carried out the coup against Boniface VIII with extraordinary daring, was a bourgeois lawyer. In the top positions of the royal council, the state system of finance, the general government of the country, townsmen were to be found—the *noblesse de la robe* as they were later called. Without the spirit formed by the new middle-class legal education, the corporations subsequently so important for France—the Parlement, the audit offices, the general provincial estates—would not have been able to exist. It was through them that the spirit of feudalism was vanquished.

Things were quite different, however, when feudalism took the upper hand at the court. But even then it could happen that in moments of deepest trouble men of the *bourgeoisie* played leading roles, as after the annihilating defeat of the French in 1356, when the king was taken prisoner by the English. The revolutionary attempt at reform by the intellectual leader of the third estate in the Estates General, ambitious as it was, remained a vain episode; it was not by chance that this intellectual leader, Étienne Marcel, was *prévôt* of the Parisian guild of merchants.

Much worse things happened when the nobility felt itself to be at the peak of its powers. In the entourage of Charles V, the French victory over the Flemish towns had exaggerated the feudal instincts and the feeling of hate towards anything bourgeois to a terrifying degree. Paris, accused of conspiracy with the Flemish towns and resistance to royal taxation demands was subjected to a seven-week reign of absolute terror. Execution without judgment, exaction of unheard-of reparations—these were the obvious things. The royal grasp extended even to the university, citadel of the intellectual culture of the city. Paris then lost its municipal constitution, of which the old merchants' guild was still the mainstay. Only the royal *Prévôt* was to carry on the government of the town. Understandably, after the experiences of 1383 the burghers of Paris supported the Duke of Burgundy, who was well disposed towards them, in his fight with the Duke of Orléans, and he gave them back what they had lost in rights. It is understandable, too, that the news of the murder of the Duke of Orléans in Paris in 1407 was received with satisfaction, and even defended by the Parisian lawyer Jean Petit as justifiable tyrannicide. However, as soon as Charles VII, a ruler of quite another stamp in terms of trustworthiness and ability, took over, the internal contact between him and the urban *bourgeoisie* was immediately re-established: the conscious aversion to English domination by the people of Paris was the necessary prerequisite for the reoccupation of Paris by royal troops. When, with the end of the war with England, the panic and distress had to some extent subsided, the desire for peace was stronger than the desire for complete autonomy. Control of finance and exploitation of the economic strength of the towns by royal taxation, practised by Louis IX and Philip the Fair, were now carried out more thoroughly. Rigid royal centralisation was again afoot which was unfavourable to the extension or indeed the retention of autonomous municipal rights. Paris and Rouen felt this in the field of trade politics; the old struggle for the monopoly of the Seine trade by one or other of the towns, which had already been practically decided in favour of Paris, was brought to an end for both towns in 1450 when Charles VII abolished both their rights of monopoly. It was however a centralisation which helped the townsmen towards economic rebuilding after all the destruction, and it increased their prosperity. In this direction the prohibition of cloth imports from the English sphere of influence had the particular effect of strongly stimulating the French cloth industry. Individual representatives of the urban *bourgeoisie* influenced and even operated the national trade and economic policies. For once again, as in the time of Philip the Fair, advisers of *bourgeois* extraction became the actual operators of the royal government, among them that great merchant Jacques Cœur, who after ten years in a leading position in the king's council became nevertheless a victim of the court nobility's hatred. However, the *bourgeois* bureaucracy remained in its dominant position.

Complete centralisation of the nation's strength was the byword in Louis XI's reign (1461–1483). His policies strengthened even more that community of interests between city and state which had been evident under Philip Augustus. Great as were the sacrifices demanded from the towns, they were used to overcome the hated feudal system. For this purpose Louis depended on the monied classes of the towns, the wealthy merchants. To increase his prosperity, and to make the French economy rich and independent of other countries—these were the great new plans of this the first economist on the French throne. Many methods were employed in the achievement of this goal. They attempted to cut out the Venetians, who sold a great deal to France but bought very little from her, by means of a direct sea connection with Alexandria— if all else failed, by force. In order to keep in the country the large sums swallowed up by the purchase of Italian silks, particularly costly brocades, the king's special policy was to make Lyons into a large-scale experimental place for the introduction of the Italian silk industry (1466) and, as the town proved recalcitrant, Tours was subsequently chosen. In 1480 the silkworkers' guild of Tours received its charter. The guild comprised twenty-two Italians, one Greek, two Burgundians and seventeen Frenchmen already trained in the industry. But in the first half of the sixteenth century 800 independent masters and 3,000–4,000 apprentices proved how successful the attempt had been to transplant a foreign industry into the country through national initiative. It was made impossible to visit the Geneva fairs; but the Lyons fairs were encouraged in every way. Trade agreements were formed with northern seafaring nations like Holland and Flanders, and also with the German Hansa. A treaty with England in 1475 finally liquidated the former state of war in the field of trade. Obviously the effects of what for the first time was such an unusual and economic policy favoured mainly the French towns and their burghers; but the broad initiative for it had already shifted to the monarchy.

In a rigidly organised state the French *bourgeoisie* recovered uncommonly swiftly from the terrible devastation of the English wars. Certainly its autonomous rights in the field of jurisdiction and government melted before the methodical advance of royal power like snow under the sun; in some towns at that time the mayors were little more than creatures of the royal government. It would however be shortsighted to gauge the mayors' position from the slight measure of self-government that still remained to them. What autonomous rights they forfeited during the course of the Middle Ages served only to strengthen the state. What the *bourgeoisie* lost in local power it won back through participation in the general government of the state. Until the beginning of Francis I's reign a preponderance of *bourgeois* advisers in the royal council was the rule. On the threshold of the new age trade was in the process of unhindered development in these towns; the Italian wars of their kings tended rather to further this internal development than to damage it. The French *bourgeoisie* around 1500 knew the value of belonging to the state; hence the particularly royal disposition of the *bonnes villes*. The towns were absorbed into a higher national unity which gave them the firm, unconditional support of national power.

The formation of the relationship between city and state in England led to a quite similar result; here the net gain finally recorded on the balance sheet of the Middle Ages in England was the more important because in no subsequent period of English history was it so much in danger as in France. The difference that this monarchy must have made to the towns at a very early date (as compared, for example, to Germany or even France) may be gauged by a matter which was of special importance to the towns— already under Henry II (1154–1189) the crown had the exclusive right to mint coins, and the whole process was centralised on London, an event which in France only occurred in 1262, while in Germany this right devolved upon the innumerable territories. Certainly this did not resolve all the problems of coinage in England. The bad currency relationships of the Continent became dangerous when the hard English currency flowed abroad and conversely the less valuable continental currencies found their way into England. But what a different relationship this economic circumstance must have produced between the cities and the state in England, compared with Germany! The same holds true for matters of weights and measures, and also customs. At the end of the twelfth century the Englishman in Germany was astonished by the innumerable Rhine taxes which seemed to him to be a frightful bit of German nonsense; no wonder, for in his own country nobody had to pay any internal taxes within the kingdom.

For the English townsmen the problem of city and state consisted in the formation of relationships with such a monarchy. From the twelfth century onwards these still underpopulated towns which with the exception of London were behind continental towns in

their development, made strong efforts in the direction of autonomy, for which oligarchic municipal committees were responsible
(such as the twelve portmen of Ipswich) which first appeared in
1200. However, even in these English towns it was the merchants'
guild, which there included a wide circle of inhabitants involved in
commerce, that was the actual representative of urban community
concerns; and even when, as in London, it played no such role in
constitutional matters—the real burgess leaders were here, as
elsewhere, the small groups of families grown rich through trade.
Their most important aim was firstly, through farming the urban
revenues of the lord of the town (and thus mainly the king's), to
gain control of taxes and then to be able themselves to elect the
municipal officials. A special municipal court was also acquired by
royal privilege. But in none of these fields did it ever succeed in
supplanting the royal power. Fundamentally the king's authority
remained unconditionally supreme, and not only in the sphere of
law but also in that of government and even of economy. Since in
the English towns there had never been any room for a movement
towards urban autonomy that might in any way be dangerous for
the crown, the latter was able very early to support the oligarchic
movement within the towns. If any abuse occurred, the monarchy
could intervene, as it did in 1206 when King John appointed a commission of twenty-four men in London to obviate the danger of
riots which had been sparked off by the taxation policies of the
people of rank towards the poorer sectors of the population. The
danger of losing the king's favour by some mistake—perhaps
insignificant in itself—and thus endangering offices and privileges,
even hung over a town like London. Obviously this monarchy was
in firm possession of a whole number of rights which continental
monarchies had either entirely or temporarily let slip through
their fingers; no English town could have envisaged minting its
own currency. However much, in the field of trade systems in
general, it may have been the municipal council's job to authorise
guilds, in London there were royal guild charters; and although
even in London municipal surveillance of trade was not out of the
question in normal times, nevertheless this made not the slightest
difference to the fact that the king's authority could intervene at

any time as a last resort. Struggles for power in the towns such as raged on the Continent between noble families and guilds were for this reason as good as non-existent in England; royal authority functioned as an arbitrator between dignitaries and guilds.

But however much the individual towns lost on autonomous rights compared with the Continent, so much the more was gained by the English towns, or more exactly by the upper class of the towns, in direct influence on the destinies of their state by means of the parliament. Ever since the model Parliament of 1295 the English townsmen had been politically represented. From this time onwards the importance of the part played by the Commons in the destiny of England continued to increase. As an individual unit, the town was able to arrive at a state of autonomous independence in relation to the king; nevertheless the latter was dependent on the goodwill of the towns' representatives in the Commons. And not only on account of their grants of money, but because he needed them as allies against the powers of the House of Lords. This was the reason why the monarchy was constantly prepared to support the oligarchy of dignitaries in the towns, in the same way that the latter expected the assurance of their privileged position with regard to the lower classes of the towns through royal support. It was the special constitutional circumstances of the country that united the English monarchy and burgher upper middle class in a firm community of interests. But even the peers, except during the savage violence of the Wars of the Roses, lacked the extreme animosity found in the opposition of nobility and burghers that developed on the Continent. For the upper middle class did not restrict itself to the town, but stood in close association with the neighbouring propertied lesser nobility, combining with them in that social community exclusive to England, the 'gentry', with the elasticity natural to it which united the respected merchant with younger sons of peers, so long as the individual members of this never-exclusive class were able and willing to belong to it. The highly important contribution made to the gentry by the middle classes was the lasting sympathy with commercial life which in England was not incompatible with the way of life of the leading social class. This was in direct contrast with continental viewpoints.

Such was the character of the *bourgeoisie* that enjoyed the long period of peace beginning with Tudor rule in 1485. It was not that the Tudors were the first to take political action in the field of economy and trade to further the economic rise of the English burghers. As early as 1258 it was believed that prohibiting the export of wool would encourage the domestic wool industry; but this and further attempts proved premature. The royal ordinance of 1381 that Englishmen might only dispatch their wares in English ships, on pain of confiscation, was only significant as an early anticipation of the same measures carried out in a time more ripe for their operation. More important was the foundation laid by Edward III in the middle of the fourteenth century for England's transition to the production of quality cloths at home; the method was to transplant Flemish weavers to England. As much as the English merchant, particularly the wool merchant, had to gain under Edward, the king was still far too dependent on foreigners and their credit; particularly in connection with the French wars, a purely fiscal viewpoint dominated the government's politico-commercial measures. It was a question of when the monarchy would use its real power to intervene in the entire commercial life of the country, in the sense of working together with the healthily egotistical, insular instincts of the strongly developing home commerce. As early as 1436 the *Libel of English Policy*, written from the point of view of the English foreign trader, had proposed a close alliance of such a nature to the monarchy. It ran:

> For yef marchaundes were cherysshede to here spede,
> We were not lykele to fayle in ony nede,
> Yff they be riche, than in prosperité
> Shal be oure londe, lordes and comonté.

With the end of the war the House of Tudor engaged in this alliance. Not without reason has the first Tudor, Henry VII, been called burgher-king. Such a cooperation was not always the case under the Tudors—not even of the particularly oustanding Tudors, Henry VII, Henry VIII, and Elizabeth. But this must not be allowed to overshadow what was important for world history— that during the time of the Tudors the monarchy led the state, and at least did not hinder the foreign-trading merchants, in that the latter grew together with the state into that active, irresistible community which laid the firm foundations for the great rise of English power in the following centuries. The English victory over the Spanish Armada in 1588, towards the end of the Tudor period, was symbolic of this close community of destiny: England would never have won this victory if all the energies of the nation had not always behaved in the manner required for such a community, selflessly putting themselves completely at the disposal of the Tudors who for a hundred years had furthered their cause, or at least let them alone. What the burghers gained from this alliance cannot be more clearly seen and admired than in a comparison of the years of 1350 and 1580. In 1350 there was still a preponderance of trade in foreign hands in the land which in the size, population and importance of its towns was way behind the Continent, particularly Germany; in 1580 the expulsion of foreign merchants from England had been accomplished, as also the transition to an active economic penetration of those countries which once had been commercially superior to her, above all Germany.

Thus the circle is complete. Only by a more exact knowledge of the development of the relationships between city and state in other European countries can one properly understand what happened in Germany. Certainly we could have taken a look at the Iberian peninsula and Scandinavia; in pre-Hapsburg Spain the relationship of monarchy and towns was a very close one, and the glorious periods of a town like Lisbon were closely connected with the great national overseas development of Portugal. In Sweden the towns began their rise in the middle of the thirteenth century, helped along by a systematic policy of the Folkunger, though certainly not without a great deal of assistance from Germany. In particular, one may mention Gustav Vasa, who at the beginning of the sixteenth century attempted to develop the merchant bodies of his towns in connection with his mercantile plans in the conscious struggle against the German Hansa—that community of towns and burghers which up to that time had more or less dominated Sweden's economy.

The German merchant's position with regard to his English

counterpart was made more difficult by a commercial factor: the strength of the German Hansa lay in intermediary trade, particularly the exchange of Western European manufactured goods for eastern raw materials. The English merchant on the other hand, after first having to make his way laboriously upwards under the shadow of foreign trade in England, had as the firm basis of his trading activities the valuable home-produced wool, and, since the fourteenth century, the very valuable cloth woven in his own country. But this fact alone is by no means sufficient to explain the complete reversal in the relationship of English and Hanseatic trade which occurred definitively in the time of Elizabeth. Until far into the fourteenth century it had been an advantage for the German towns that, almost completely independent as they were of centralised power, they could go their own way in complete economic freedom, particularly abroad. But from the fifteenth century the relationship between German city and state became the towns' undoing. In the later Middle Ages the solid power of a national state stood behind the English towns, as it did also in France. This close connection with a strong central power was not forthcoming in Germany, because such a power no longer existed at the time. Nothing could make good this deficiency; not even the economic strength of the German towns, which was thoroughly superior to the English in 1400, nor the highest diplomatic efforts, which at the peace of Utrecht in 1473 brought a sigh from the English negotiator John Russell, who, outclassed in the diplomatic game, remarked that he 'would rather negotiate with all the princes in the world than with envoys of the Hanseatic council'. Least helpful of all was the form of state which developed more and more in Germany after 1400—that of independent territories. For these became one of the greatest dangers that threatened the German town of the late Middle Ages. And so, on account of the fateful development of the German state, the towns of Germany were holding out in a lost outpost from the end of the Middle Ages. All too visible was the contrast between the splendid cultural blossoming of the rise of the towns and the simultaneous decline of national power in Germany, and it is a bad thing when cultural and national development become as divorced as they were in Germany at that time. The result could only be that the towns were dragged into the national decline, and became inferior to those towns which had national power behind them. Thus the English merchant of the sixteenth century took over not only the position of the German merchant in England, but penetrated victoriously into the German economic zone, which had become thoroughly fragile. Perhaps nowhere else is the decisive importance of the state as a causal factor even of the formation of cultural conditions—and not only in the field of commerce—so directly and convincingly displayed as in the entirely divergent paths taken by German and English urban development between the twelfth and the sixteenth centuries.

11   Seal of the City of Stockholm

4

THE CITY
BETWEEN THE EMPIRE AND
THE NATIONAL STATES

❋

Decisive as was the formation of their political relationships for the history of the towns of the great European nations, one of the most important centres of European urban civilisation lay not within, but between, the great nations of France and England, and the German *regnum* which gradually disintegrated in the late Middle Ages. It had not always been so. There were no empty spaces between the kingdoms that succeeded the empire of Charlemagne. The Scheldt formed the boundary between the eastern and western kingdoms after the buffer state of Lothar had disappeared. The princely powers east of the Scheldt were connected with the German king by the oath of homage, those of the west with the King of France. Up to the eleventh century the emperor exercised the imperial rights in the lands east of the Scheldt, although conversely, the influence of the weak French king on the left bank of the Scheldt was really ineffectual, particularly in Flanders. But around 1200 the picture changed entirely. Real imperial supremacy was no more. In Lorraine power relationships were formed independently of the concept of empire—a concept which was losing all its political meaning and giving way to powerful secular states, particularly to the Duchy of Brabant. Philip Augustus' victory at Bouvines in August 1214 hit hardest the Count of Flanders, the ally of the English king. In spite of this France only succeeded in tearing away the southern parts, and not the whole, of the county of Flanders from the emergent feudal state and integrating them into the French national system. One of the reasons for this fact, which has been of historical importance up to the present day, and therefore cannot be overlooked, was the character of Flemish towns.

The relationship between the Flemish state—represented by the Count of Flanders and his officials—and the Flemish towns, was unique in its time. Independence of France and the excellence of the Flemish counts had, as early as the twelfth century, brought this French feudal county to a height of political maturity in its political organisation that had been achieved nowhere else in Europe at the time, not even in Sicily or later in 'royal' France at the end of the reign of Philip Augustus. The county of Flanders would never have been able to attain such an importance if it had been an agricultural nation. Its disproportionately great political strength was due to the intensity of its urban commerce. Bruges and Ghent, Ypres and Arras, Douai and Lille—to mention only the most important—together with other towns within a relatively small space, created the first centre of a North European textile industry which supplied the world market of the time, and whose absolute and relative importance cannot be too highly stressed. In our first chapter we indicated the close connection between an emergent urban civilisation and trade, and Flanders represents that portion of Europe where this connection found its highest expression. The early trader, still restlessly roving hither and thither, who discovered for Flanders the quality of English wool, settled in Flanders with his trade and travelling companions in a merchants' settlement under the protection of some noble's castle, brought about the transference of the rural weaving trade into the new towns, accustomed them to the spinning of English wool, made them dependent on himself for their business by means of an early-developed system of advances and won the whole of Europe as a market for their products—this merchant was the real creator of the Flemish town. Thus the merchant element here dominated the life of the town right from the start, in a way that is only paralleled in the large German towns founded in the twelfth century. But the Low Countries also had that older type of German town, the episcopal town whose inhabitants were far more dependent on their main consumers—the bishop and his spiritual entourage. This was particularly the case with Liège. Here political dependence was added to economic dependence; it is not by chance that the episcopal towns of Cambrai and Liège were the scenes of far more serious struggles between the population of the towns and their lords than are familiar to us in the Rhenish episcopal towns. But it was otherwise with those young Flemish merchants' towns, whose first beginnings as merchants' towns—and not as the strongholds of counts—go back as far as the eleventh and even the tenth century and which then flourished so wonderfully from the twelfth century onwards. Their relationship with the Count of Flanders was fundamentally different from that of, for example, Liège with its bishop. Nowhere was the count lord of the town in the way that bishops were in their towns, where lord and townsmen had to wrestle for power within the same restricted space.

Instead there existed between the Flemish towns, already well developed around 1100, and the count, a far-reaching community of interests which made itself felt very clearly for the first time in 1128 after the murder of Charles the Good. The first French attempts at annexation came to grief because of the Flemish towns-people's resistance; the new ruling family had them to thank for the fact that it was in possession of the county. The strength of the county resided in the strength of urban commerce. Allied foreign-political interests moved towards a common destiny. The blossoming of the Flemish towns was based on the undisturbed importation of English wool; the security of the Flemish count, with regard to French ambitions for annexation, on the support of the English crown. On top of this there were, until far into the thirteenth century, internal political interests common to the towns and the count; both stood against the knightly nobility which continually tended towards France. With such a strong interdependence of count and towns, the townsmen's striving for autonomy in Flanders and the preservation of the count's share even in the government of the towns—which strengthened the political unity of the county—were able to co-exist relatively easily and without friction.

The special jury courts set up by the lord of the land for the towns actually came very soon, by virtue of their membership, to be at the disposal of a small circle of families formed by a group of notables from the upper middle class: the *poorters*. This class was made up of dealers or retailers in cloth, who were at the same time the largest property owners in the towns. In Ghent in the thirteenth century it was a circle of thirty-nine people who functioned as jurors, of whom thirteen were active for the current year, assisted by the thirteen of the previous year, while the remaining thirteen had a year off. By that time, these jurors had long since become the town council, upon which the whole internal government of the town devolved, though not, however in such a loose and uncontrolled fashion as was the case in the imperial German towns. When in the twelfth century the ruler's castellans, who were still drawn from the feudal aristocracy, were replaced by his bailiffs, who were real paid officials, it was these officials residing in the towns who pointed up the significance of the count's right of surveillance. Even if the self-government of the towns was hardly affected, there was always a possibility of intervention, and furthermore the fact that jurors were sworn in by representatives of the count served as a control over the people involved in the government of the town. Moreover, there was the constitutional principle that none of the higher courts, even the municipal jury court, could sit in the absence of the bailiff. The political strength and commercial solidity of the county were also very clearly expressed in the uniform and well-ordered system of currency. The counts also had, for the time, an unusually far-reaching trade and commercial policy, which was often more liberal towards foreigners than the towns would have liked. The constitutional situation which had been reached remained intact—with some exceptions— as long as the count and the upper middle class of the towns felt themselves to be mutually dependent by virtue of their old community of interests in economic and foreign policy, and in any case up to the end of the thirteenth century.

What had been achieved, commercially, in the Flemish towns, was rivalled only by the towns of northern Italy. In their specialised field of cloth production they were unequalled. Nothing bears better witness to the uniqueness of their industry than the fact that the similarly highly developed Florentine cloth trade attempted to imitate the cloths of Flemish towns such as Ypres, Douai and Arras, and that Flemish cloths were an article of trade in the Orient. After Bruges became the continental trading centre for English wool around 1300, the position of monopoly enjoyed by the Flemish cloth industry was consolidated even further. The volume of production, already significant in the thirteenth century, increased further at the beginning of the fourteenth. The number of lead seals which Ypres had attached to the cloths manufactured by its weavers as checking marks rose from 10,500 in 1306 to 92,500 in 1313, although the threat of political entanglements with France reduced this number considerably in the following years. The number of pieces of Flemish cloth which in 1368 found their way from Hamburg via Oldesloe to Lübeck ran to at least 23,000 and that year was troubled by the war with Waldemar of Denmark. It is significant that the merchants who carried the Flemish cloth eastwards from Bruges were entirely German, and mainly from Lübeck. The Bruges merchant, who in the thirteenth century still marketed his own wares abroad, had as good as given up this practice since merchants were to be found in Bruges from the whole of Europe, buying and selling there. Since direct dealing between one foreign trader and another was strictly forbidden in Bruges, a comfortable profit was assured for the Bruges merchant. Through his hands went the entire turnover of goods in Bruges itself. Apart from this the *poorter* of Bruges was also a retailer in the local cloth trade, a further very important source of his prosperity.

A measure of the prosperity of Flemish cloth production is the large range of qualities that were available. The numerous local names signifying places of origin, very common in the Middle Ages, also indicated different qualities; apart from this, within the same town, particularly the big towns, various kinds were produced. Individual towns had adapted their production to certain specialities. Thus Bruges produced the *saie*, a light stuff of fine wool. Arras, too, produced a light weave, the *rasch*, a word that would seem to indicate its place of origin. The scarlet industry was centred in Ghent. It happened too that places which produced

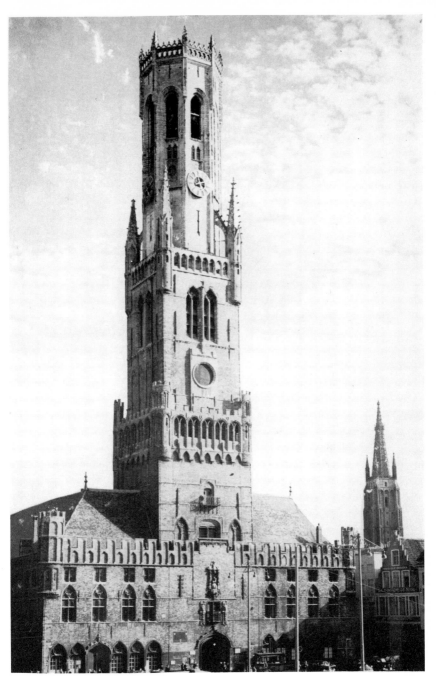

12 Bruges: the 'Old Hall', the late thirteenth-century Guildhall

13   Bruges: the 'great crane'
From Bayerisches Staatsbibliothek, Munich, Cod. lat. 23638, f. 11v.

goods of lower quality imitated the more highly prized quality of a neighbouring town. Thus in 1392 Ypres warned the Hanseatic emissaries meeting in Bruges of a cheap imitation of Ypres cloth (*laken*) in Ghent. The Novgorod trading post had to complain about Popering *laken*, which was made like that of Valenciennes, around 1350. The variation in quality was reflected by variations in trade. In the first half of the fourteenth century the firm of the brothers Gallin carried on for decades a trade of wholesale cloth buying in Flanders, but specialised almost exclusively in the cheap Popering cloth, selling it in large parcels of up to 100 pieces (averaging twenty-five yards in length) by a business agreement to merchants in Lübeck, who then resold it in the Baltic countries. A merchant like Johann Wittenborg preferred better-quality stuff around 1359.

Evidently Bruges was the place of export for the cloth, but the raw materials—English, and later Spanish wool—also found their way via Bruges to the Flemish weavers' workshops. Just how far the English connection preponderated in the foreign trade of Bruges can be seen in the fact that the jurymen of Bruges could only be elected out of the London Hansa, that is, the Flemish merchants' foreign trade organisation that dealt with London. When towards the end of the thirteenth century the independent trade of Bruges with England declined, the London Hansa disappeared along with it. But Bruges became the continental depot for English wool. Apart from the Flemish cloth manufacturers, merchants from the south also met their requirements of English raw wool in Bruges, even though this led to friction with the Flemings, who would have liked to see the working of English wool confined solely to Flanders. Even in Nuremberg about 1360 a merchant like Ulmann Stromer knew exactly what the dealings were in Bruges with regard to English wool.

Foreign merchants were much preferred who took cloth with them from Bruges and not wool, and brought with them goods from their own countries. They came from the whole of Europe. Dutchmen and Frisians brought the products of their own economy —grain and horses, cattle and herrings. Further eastwards there was no town of the Hansa which was not in some way interested in the

Bruges traffic; for most of them, and above all the Hansa as a whole, it was the most important trading place of all. Cologne and Brunswick, Soest and Dortmund, Lüneburg and Bremen, Stendal and Salzwedel, Magdeburg and Erfurt—to pick out only a few of the towns west of the Elbe—were represented in Bruges by their merchants and their most important products.

The most significant and prominent role in the Flemish-Hanseatic traffic belonged to Hamburg and Lübeck; at the same time they acted as agents for the exchange of goods between Flanders and the whole of the Baltic area. This is connected with what we said in the second chapter about the origins and the commercial nature of the Hansa. From the Flemish point of view, what the German Hansa had done for itself became very clear; it has been of decisive importance for the history of European trade that in the thirteenth century the Flemish retail trade with the east fell off, and that the German merchant, who had become powerful in the Baltic, took over the supply of all goods from Flanders eastwards. Its monopoly in eastern trade made the Hansa in Flanders the respected, and in certain circumstances the dreaded power which, under the energetic leadership of Lübeck, could force its will upon Flanders by means of trade barriers and the methods of economic warfare. But such trials of strength were the exception. The rule was that between the Hansa on one side and the count and the towns of Flanders on the other a situation existed which rested on mutual appreciation and the dictates of complementary commercial interests which was advantageous for both parties, and which was only shaken when the foundations of both parties' prosperity were deeply affected. Until that time the trade privileges granted to the Hansa by the count and the towns of Flanders provided, with their obligation to deposit Hanseatic goods for sale in Bruges and only in Bruges, what was necessary to make Flanders trade complete. One would have to count up all the Baltic towns to enumerate all the towns that had a direct or indirect interest in the trade with Bruges. The greater the incidence of the journey from the Baltic to the North Sea around Jutland, the greater the interest of the eastern towns, above all Riga, in Bruges. Apart from the Hanseatic towns, the trade deputies of the Teutonic Order were very welcome guests there. It was mainly through Hanseatic supply that Swedish ore reached Bruges.

But with all this, we only see one side of the traffic centred on Bruges. Northern France, which itself possessed an excellent cloth industry, especially after Arras, St Omer and Aire fell to France in 1200 and 1212—Lille, Douai and Béthune followed a hundred years later—had no great need to turn to Bruges. But it was different with western France; here, French wine exports and Flemish cloth exports complemented each other excellently. La Rochelle, the Bordeaux of the Middle Ages, saw many a Flemish ship, but also many a Spanish one, on its way to Bruges, stopping off in the harbour to replenish its freight. In 1350 no less than forty Spanish ships arrived on the Swin, the roadstead of Bruges, in the early summer. Their main cargoes were Spanish fruits and iron, silk from Granada, and, in times of tension with England, even Spanish wool. But the attraction of Bruges stretched even further. As early as the twelfth century Lombards were as active in Flanders, particularly as money-lenders, as in Arras. In the troubles at the beginning of the fourteenth century Bruges fell into debt to the great Italian banks which kept resident representatives in the town. Overland trade in goods from Italy had also developed in connection with the Champagne fairs; but it still involved Flanders as a whole rather than Bruges alone. Not until the confusion of the French wars towards the end of the thirteenth century was there any fundamental change. From the beginning of the fourteenth century the Genoan galleys came to Sluys, the seaport of Bruges, bringing cargoes, too, on behalf of the Florentines until such time as Florence, after acquiring the harbour of Leghorn, sent its own galleys northwards. Soon Venice joined Genoa, sending state-organising convoys of galleys to Bruges. In so far as the individual merchant, especially the Genoan, sent ships to Bruges, he soon went over to the more economical sailing ship. The Italian ship brought mainly Levantine goods, particularly spices, and also products of the Italian silk industry such as costly brocades for ecclesiastical robes, exquisite examples of which, having travelled from Italy to Lübeck via Bruges, may be admired in the Lübeck museum today. Flanders, however, maintained its position so well even with regard to Mediterranean products that Flemish cloth was a popular export cargo to the Mediterranean. We have already mentioned Florentine attempts at imitation.

The most lively imagination cannot picture vividly enough the life that went on in Bruges and its port. Bruges was indeed the great harbour of Europe, the place on which all the lines of commerce converged. The face of the town was decisively formed by trade. The financial sacrifices made by the *poorters* of Bruges for the improvement of the town, for public buildings and fortifications, were very considerable; the huge wall of 1297, at least seven kilometres long, swallowed up about £10,000, an expense that could only be borne with the help of the Italian bankers, the agents of the Peruzzis and the Bardis. Rich *poorters* came to the assistance of other building projects; a consortium of five people carried out in 1295 the practical and rational plan for the building of the 'New Hall', intended mainly for the largest export, cloth. The 'Old Hall' on the narrow side of the 'Great Square' was dominated in the middle of its façade by the proud belfry of the town, a symbol of its autonomy and wealth. This tower, over 240 feet high, is a dominant feature of the town; still in the main creation of the grandiose building undertaken by the people of Bruges at the end of the thirteenth century, it was added to in the fifteenth with a further towering storey. English wool, Bruges' most important import, was bought and sold in a special wool house, in which the Flemings themselves were the principal merchants. Spanish wool, insofar as it found its way for some special reason to Bruges, was to be found separated from the English on the ground floor of the spice hall. Here were stored, mainly goods from the south, by no means exclusively spices.

But it was not just a question of these splendid halls, which were as much witness of a very accurately and well-thought-out organisation of trade on the part of the government, as indications of a sense of dignity and display; there were plenty of other architectural and technical achievements to serve the same all-determining purpose. The municipal balance, converted to scales in 1282 with bowls and beams sent from Lübeck, was soon made redundant by the personal weighing machines of individual foreign merchants' associations. Special fame was accorded to the Bruges crane, driven by a treadwheel, which attracted so much attention to itself that many a Bruges painter—no less than Memling among them— made a place for it in the background of his portraits and altar pictures. A poorer cousin of the Bruges crane still stands in the old harbour district of Lüneburg. But most important was the continual working on the artery of the town, its waterway to the sea. For this too the town raised huge sums of money; in the fifteenth century all attempts to halt the silting-up were proved in vain. Nevertheless the great sluice of Bruges near Damme, through which in the previous centuries passed the sea traffic of Bruges, was a technical wonder of its time.

Ecclesiastical buildings, erected within the protection of the encircling wall, fitted in worthily with the whole with an imposing number of parish churches, and an unusual abundance of monasteries and hospitals, most of which go back to the thirteenth century.

The foreign merchants settling in Bruges did their bit to bring out the importance of trade in the architectural aspect of the town. The house which was built for the merchants of Genoa in 1399 is still kept up today. To begin with the Hanseatic merchants stayed in rooms in the Carmelite monastery; only in the fifteenth century, when the Hansa and Bruges had both already passed their primes did the Hanseatic merchants build their own meeting house. Similar centres were created by the merchants of other nations; the Italians met in the consulates of their home towns. Numerous foreign merchants rented whole houses in residential streets, whose cellars served as storehouses and display rooms. It only reflected the way of life of the distinguished Bruges merchant of the fifteenth century, orientated as it was towards the development of luxury and rich middle-class culture, if the foreign merchants also strove to shine by means of ostentation. In 1468 the individual foreign merchants' associations could be seen in the richest costumes, taking part in the procession meeting the bride of Charles the Bold—Florentines and Venetians, Spaniards and Genoans, 'Eastlings' (as the Hanseatic merchants were known in Bruges) 108 strong, accompanied by six pages. But by far more important than this pomp and finery of the streets was the fine art, dedicated to the spirit of the upper middle class of the time, of Memling or Van Eyck.

The other large Flemish towns presented a similar appearance; only here the buildings connected with harbour traffic were missing. All the more splendid were the buildings designed for the selling of cloth, among which was perhaps the most magnificent secular building of the Middle Ages in Europe—the Cloth Hall of Ypres—also dominated by a splendid belfry. The halls stretch out east and west from the belfry for 144 yards; this was the starting-place from which Ypres cloth went on its way as an article of world trade. It would be impossible to imagine a more representative and magnificent architectural reflection of the importance of the goods which the town produced for export to the world.

In its birth and in its formation the Flemish town reflected only the absolutely dominant power of trade which exercised control over everything and ruled according to its own dictates. It would be a good thing however not only to admire the proud trading halls of medieval Ypres but also to take a look at the wretched suburbs in which the population of weavers lived—in the shadow of the trade which ruled their lives, whose splendour they had to serve and whose leaders made their money from selling what the weavers produced. The dependence on the merchant class of all who worked with their hands at producing the cloth was even greater. Only the cloth merchant was the owner of the raw materials, that is, mainly the wool but frequently also the dyes. The various workers involved in weaving, even if they were master-weavers and themselves employed workers, worked only for wages with goods that belonged to other people—the merchants. This was true for the actual weavers as much as for the fullers, the dyers, the cutters, and whatever other kinds of specialists may have been involved in the preparation of cloth and wool. Moreover there was no system whereby the product that was being worked upon could be passed from one 'master' to the 'master' concerned with the subsequent process in the manufacture; after each process the goods had to be restored to the cloth merchant, who checked the work that had been done and then turned it over to another man of his choice to continue the process. Thus the cloth being made was continually going back to the business premises of the man who owned the wool, until finally he took receipt of the finished cloth which he then disposed of on the European market. If around 1300 the *skrivekamer* was the firm, permanent centre of the Hanseatic merchant's business, it was even more so for his Flemish colleague. His business house was at the same time the place from which he watched with great care over the transformation within the various technical workshops of the town, of the raw material he had bought in England, into a valuable marketable finished product. Evidently both the wool and the finished products were stored in this business house, until such time as they were taken to the public halls, either local or foreign, as for instance the cloth hall of Douai in Paris. Such a cloth merchant had enormous opportunities for gain; the manual workers who carried out the transformation of wool into cloth were poorly paid, while the cloth merchant himself drew most of the profit from the margin between the price of the raw material and the finished articles.

On top of this the political power that the cloth merchants enjoyed—as members of guilds and as jurymen—allowed them to introduce a system of public control by means of numerous inspectors, from whom the weavers and their helpers were never safe in their own homes. There was no union to form a protective buffer between the small master-weaver and the wholesale cloth merchant (all-powerful by virtue of his sole possession of the raw material), when the latter was negotiating with him about taking over work; it was entirely a matter for the merchant's whim whether or not he wished to give work to the same man again; the merchant had the economic fate of those who were involved in the production of cloth entirely in his hand. Furthermore if the small master lived in a house belonging to the merchant, worked in lieu of paying rent, was probably in debt to him or—what seldom occurred in Flanders but so much the more frequently in Florence—had pledged his sole economically useful possession, the loom, to the merchant, then there was hardly any difference at all between him and the ordinary worker who was employed, for daily wage, in the merchant's dyeing-shop. The small man, living in the shadow of a thousand worries as to where his next meal was coming from, stood at an infinite distance, socially and economically, from the entrepreneur ruthlessly striving for profit, the capitalist, who, significantly for the completely dominant role of trade in the economy of the really important medieval town, was above all a trader, organising the production of cloth to suit his activity as a trader and for his own purposes. Out of this tense situation, domestic industry developed as the organisational form of cloth production; a domestic industry in which already the evil manifestations of the system of barter appeared by which the wage-earning workers were paid in kind instead of money. The consequences of this system at their personal level were inhuman, and unbearable for the employees when they came up against a personality of such cynicism and unscrupulousness, who exploited his economic supremacy and social position of power as brutally as the Douai patrician and cloth merchant Jehan Boine Broke, of whom G. Espinas has been able to draw such an informative and completely authentic picture on the basis of unique legal documents. A *véritable bandit industriel*—such was this man, for whom the idea of a 'fair price' was nothing more than a joke. Certainly Jehan Boine Broke may not have been typical of his class. But this refers only to the use he made of the system, not to the system itself; this was general practice.

Nor did that sector of the upper class which was no longer active in the cloth trade and manufacture, but had retired to live in luxury on a private income, subscribe any less to the idea of keeping the lower classes down. The ostentation of this circle embittered the poor man; the particularly French manner which this upper class affected more and more in the thirteenth century helped to sharpen the social contrasts still further. Apart from this there is obviously a close connection between the emergence of a powerful sector of propertied people within the upper middle class, which disposed of the membership of the juries and thus of the whole town, and the serious budgetary crises which the Flemish towns had to go through towards the end of the thirteenth century. In order to avoid the dubious assistance of Italian financial

14   Guild officials taking the oath
From an Olmütz MS. of 1440

15 Seal of the City of Ypres,
late thirteenth century

16 Ypres: the thirteenth-century
Cloth Hall (rebuilt after the First
World War)

aid they turned to taxes, which did not affect the propertied upper class but, to a disproportionally large extent, the mass of the small people. Contemporary satire quite clearly accuses the upper classes of the most evil policy over the exaction of taxes which, wherever possible, were farmed by other people of their rank. There appeared to be nothing, as far as this already declining upper class was concerned, that could not be demanded of the small man; the *Keure* of Ghent wanted the abductor of the daughter of a poor man to go unpunished. Great as had been its merit at one time, the behaviour of this leading class that was sinking in a sea of pride, arrogance, epicureanism and self-interest was completely unbearable. Its hour had come.

It came, as is the rule in such tense situations, in connection with the conflicts of the external political situation, the influence of which on the urban life of Flanders have found in Pirenne their unrivalled chronicler. Certainly, the first great uprising of 1280, which spread quickly over the Flemish towns, was of a purely internal kind. Its aim was the deposition of the hated patricians in favour of the oppressed classes, that is, above all, the manual workers. Here, as also in the later troubles in German towns, they were joined by merchants whose rise to political and economic leadership was obstructed by the conscious restriction of power by the upper class to the smallest possible circle of people. But the political conditions of Flanders were far too advanced for a dispute between upper class and manual workers to have been possible in isolation. The Count of Flanders and his bailiffs welcomed this opportunity which forced them to intervene. Very soon the danger of losing their former far-reaching independence to the bailiffs troubled the upper classes more than the dispute within the population of the town itself; the merchants who had helped the workers' movement of 1280 splintered off in order to allow the upper class to re-establish the earlier municipal freedoms. Nevertheless, the power of the leading families was weaker than before 1280; it was a sign of their weakness that they looked around for assistance against the count's designs, only to find it in a way which was basically only bent on replacing the influence of the Flemish count with a certainly no less painful bureaucratic domination in the towns themselves—the French king, feudal lord of the Count of Flanders.

With all this, the intra-urban struggles over the right of workers to form corporations, in other words the formation of autonomous bodies within individual trades, and their part in the exercise of power, had become tied up with the great political struggles of the states, firstly between Flanders and France and then between the dynastic houses of Flanders themselves, and finally, with the great struggle between France and England, in which the Flemish towns were essentially pawns in the game. The changing alliances of the groups in the struggles within the towns with those of the contesting states enlivened the history of Flanders with an abundance of dramatic occurrences, individually confusing, but by which the life of the towns was continually affected and shaken to its foundations.

This was particularly true of the famous battle of Courtrai, in which the urban upper class stood for France and the small man for the house of the Count of Flanders. It was because of this resistance that the French attempt to annexe the County of Flanders foundered. Thus this battle has influenced the map of Europe in a very important place up to the present day. What the small man had hoped to gain was twofold: economically, to break his complete dependence on the cloth merchant's guilds; and politically, to win power in the town. Both expectations were very imperfectly fulfilled. It was of little use to the weavers that directly after the battle they were assured of a complete freedom of trade, in other words that in principle they had the right to buy and sell cloth. Not even the disappearance of the hated guilds from the Flemish towns had any real effect on the weavers' economic situation. Their dependence on the guilds disappeared; in its place there was their dependence on capital, on those who were in a position to buy raw material regularly and in sufficient bulk, and who then alone were able to sell the cloth in bulk. Imagine a Lübeck merchant who by a business agreement disposed of Flemish cloth in Lübeck itself in quantities of up to a hundred pieces having to buy it all in Flanders off small master-weavers! Bulk trade had become by far and away the dominant form in the Flemish cloth trade, even in its subsidiary enterprises, and a changeover to 'professional trade' was not at all possible. The fact was that the Flemish weaving industry was not an industry producing for the local market, but one geared to international commerce, with all the advantages and all the disadvantages of such a situation. Only the advantages accrued to the cloth dealers and retailers, and the disadvantages to those who were engaged in manufacturing the cloth and who never succeeded in rising to that economic independence which the other workers took for granted.

For this reason alone it was improbable that full political power in the town would ever devolve upon the unions. It was, however, a real gain for the weavers that they were now able to have a corporate constitution, which the ruling class up to that time had attempted to suppress by all the means available. Apart from this the towns of Flanders and Brabant offer examples of the most varied solutions. In the towns of Brabant, principally Brussels and Louvain, the confused entanglements of Flanders in foreign affairs had no effect, and the upper class was pleased to bow before their lord if only it could be assured of his protection from a rising on the part of the weavers, which threatened to happen even there. For this reason the dominance of the upper class was maintained here, and the guilds completely controlled the cloth industry, until the end of the century, when they allowed the unions to have a share in government. The dominance of the upper class in Liège was broken in 1313; later the bishop, as lord, brought about a distribution of the municipal offices between workers and upper-class families; this lasted until 1384 when the upper class, quite different here and closely related to the rural nobility, renounced its share in government, leaving the unions which here were made up of real manual labourers, and not weavers, to exercise political power. What happened in Flanders itself was less peaceful and was indeed responsible for bloodshed.

The Flemish towns as a whole after the battle of Courtrai won an unusual increase in power: at that time Bruges, Ypres and Ghent were in a position to exercise real power over the whole of Flanders, in that each of these towns subjected the surrounding countryside, and also the smaller neighbouring towns, to an ever-increasing domination. As the weavers in these towns acquired influence, they energetically saw to it that no rural weaving industry should rise up that might be harmful to them; the safest means of preventing this was to destroy the country looms. Even the smaller towns had to resign themselves to brutal oppression on the part of the three large ones: Bruges destroyed Sluys, Ypres caused the downfall of the Popering weaving industry, Ghent ruined Dendermonde. In the fourteenth century Flanders was not far from splitting up into three city-states, each dominating the land around it. What prevented this was the quarrels between the towns themselves, which caused them to side with very different political factions, and which thus finally saved the ruling power of the count. But the disunity between the three big towns was mainly determined by the disunity of their own leaders. This was the reason for the defeat of the rising of coastal Flanders, kindled by Bruges, which came to a bloody end at the battle of Cassel in 1328; Ghent, at that time dominated by the upper class, was on the opposite side. Jakob van Artevelde, the real leader of Ghent at the time of the Anglo-French war, when Ghent, in direct opposition to the Count of Flanders, made a public alliance with England, met his death in 1345 through a weavers' plot; the weavers in Bruges and Ypres were overpowered by the other unions in their turn. Ghent, isolated as it was, still dominated and defended only by weavers, succumbed in 1349. And with it went once again all the hopes of the weavers in the Flemish towns. Many of them preferred to leave the country and settle in England, taking their skill with them to the country with the best wool production. They thus laid the foundations for the rise of the English cloth industry, then about to begin—the rise of the most dangerous competitor as far as Flemish commercial greatness was concerned.

The growing English cloth industry had as yet little effect. Flanders was actually going through the period of its highest prosperity up to about 1370 in the fields of trade and of cloth manufacture. But the tensions within the towns had by no means diminished—on the contrary. The count's policy in the countryside, favouring it as a counterbalance to the towns, encouraged the rural weaving industry at the expense of the urban weavers. The urban upper class of cloth dealers however was able to come to good terms with the rural weaving industry; it simply meant that their opportunities for profit were increased. The same was true for the real manual workers who had nothing to do with the weavers. The result was a renewed sharpening of social contrasts and of the hate the poor people bore to the rich. The latter were now prepared to accommodate the growing power of the count within their old desires for urban self-government, provided only that he protected them from the daily threat of outbreaks of fury among the mass of weavers. But if outbreaks in fact occurred, they were necessarily also directed against the count; thus the weavers could boast that they were the last defenders of urban freedom against subjection to the count. When in 1379 a sudden weavers' rising put first Ghent and subsequently Bruges and Ypres in the weavers' power, the count's supremacy was again severely tested. He needed French help in order to deliver a crushing blow to the rioters—this was the significance of the battle of Roosebeke in 1382. Ghent itself, which in these years had riveted the eyes of Europe on its unprecedented displays of strength, remained on its feet in spite of the defeat. It was the new lord of the land, Philip of Burgundy, who, in 1385, first managed to get the town amicably on the road leading to recognition of his sovereign rights.

The beginning of the rule of the House of Burgundy marks the end of the period of the most bloody political and social struggles that the history of the European town has ever seen over such a small area. The Burgundians had no difficulty in integrating the Flemish towns into the state. Attempts at revolt such as occurred in 1437 in Bruges and in 1451 in Ghent, given the decline of community spirit amongst the Flemish towns, had only local significance, were easily suppressed and, furthermore, cost the towns their rights of supremacy which they had claimed over the surrounding countryside. The time was past when the towns as a whole or individual classes within their populations could side with or against the ruler, with or against England or France. The gruesome, weeks-long, systematic destruction of the town of Liège and its inhabitants in 1468, and the contemptuous annihilation of the privileges of the town of Brussels in the following year were the drastic methods that Charles the Bold employed to let even the Flemish towns know that, in face of the new ruling power, supported by quite different military strengths, there was no longer such a thing as independent town politics.

When Flanders was integrated with the Burgundian states, not only was the heroic time of the social and constitutional struggles of its towns over. The foundations of their economic existence were already threatened. The fifteenth century saw the irresistible decline of the Flemish cloth industry. English wool, its most important basis, became scarce, and was deliberately made more difficult to acquire by the English; Spanish wool was an inadequate substitute. English cloth exports correspondingly increased. Ypres was hit the hardest; the decrease in its population in the fifteenth century was irresistible, though in spite of this in 1486 a third of the reduced population is said to have sought its living by begging. Ghent tried to maintain itself by a reckless exploitation of its corn stocks and gradually found a certain substitute in the linen industry; Brussels became the residence of one of the richest European princely courts whose luxury requirements gave a living to many. Bruges made every effort to maintain itself as a place of trade and finance. If one wished to draw any conclusion from the architectural achievements of the town in the fifteenth century, one might plump for economic prosperity; but the same thing applied here as frequently elsewhere, particularly in the German towns—the town only got its finest and richest buildings when it had already gone beyond the peak of its economic development. Whoever in 1450 wanted to see a strongly flourishing town life no longer steered his ship to the Swin but to the Scheldt, to Antwerp. With small coercive measures of various kinds Bruges, whose commercial spirit was showing signs of age, attempted to save its position—as though its dwindling force of attraction could have been maintained by means of ordinances. The English merchants had their house in Antwerp as early as 1407. Italians and Spaniards followed. The Eastlings, the Hanseatic merchants, joined them hesitantly, and too late. Their fate was inextricably bound up with that of Flanders.

Flanders and the Hansa had blossomed in the closest mutual

connection; occasional disturbances of the agreement which could lead to suspension of trade and economic war had no effect on the existence of this community of interests which found its mutually useful expression in the centre at Bruges. Both shared the same enemy, which threatened to destroy the bases of their economy— the Englishman with his cloth exports. Both would have gladly fixed, by means of protectionist measures, the conditions of an already half-gone age in a present that was so much less favourable to both. The Hanseatic merchants had to join in if they did not want to be excluded from the new commercial centre on the Scheldt. The silting-up of the Swin at the end of the fifteenth century and warlike developments in Flanders did their bit to take away from Bruges the position it had gloriously held for around 300 years.

Protected and helped by the Burgundian state, safeguarded by a well-balanced distribution of power within the town, Antwerp did everything to make the stay of the foreign merchant, who in any case came to the town for his own benefit, as pleasant as humanly possible. It allowed him a degree of commercial freedom hardly known in Bruges, which was paralysed with protectionism. In this matter, too, the town and the national government went hand in hand. Although the Antwerpers themselves were prominent neither in seafaring nor in the goods trade, but rather, like the *poorters* of Bruges, rather made their own profits out of the international merchant life of the town, as brokers, hirers of storehouses and residences, and soon also as bankers and commission agents, they nevertheless avoided trying to limit the exercise of the brokers' profession to members of a corporation, or otherwise encroaching upon the foreign merchants' freedom of activity. Their success was enormous. It was out of the completely free traffic that existed between the foreign merchants that the first modern stock exchange grew. The stream of goods in the direction of Antwerp was greatly enlivened by the large shipments of Indian spices, for which Portugal was responsible; the South Germans enriched trade with copper, metal goods and fustian. International money and exchange business reached a volume unknown before that time. While the Hanseatic merchant faded into the background the South German merchant, particularly the Augsburger, played a correspondingly more significant role there. Venice, Florence, Bruges and the Hansa fell behind simultaneously; Lisbon, Lyon, Antwerp and the South German towns enjoyed a corresponding rise. Still far off were the fateful years of the Spanish plundering of Antwerp in 1576 and 1585 by which not only the town's prosperity but also the South German merchant, weakened by the national bankruptcy of the time, were annihilated. The latter's ties with Antwerp were to be a community of fate for him, as had been the case before with the Hansa and Bruges.

When Antwerp was moving swiftly towards its peak at the end of the Middle Ages, Amsterdam was still a place of modest importance, according to general European estimation. But already at that time this town had two important advantages over Antwerp, which were to make her surpass Antwerp around a hundred years later; firstly a flourishing indigenous trade, and secondly, an important shipping line of her own in the service of which the rural and the fishing populations of Holland and Zealand offered a very strong reserve of daring, and sea-going experience. The Dutch shipping, particularly that centred on Amsterdam, pushed itself into the already existing foreign connections as freight shipping for foreign merchants; firstly into Flemish-English shipping, which mainly carried the wool traffic between England and Flanders, and then into the traffic lines of Hanseatic trade involved in the import of beer from Hamburg and above all corn from the Baltic. The freight shipper soon turned into the independent trader who now fetched grain from the Baltic ports on his own account, and on top of this was in the happy position of having an excellent bulk article in the form of French sea salt ready-made for him for the journey eastwards. Amsterdam was already distinguished by a flourishing trade in corn in the fifteenth century; in the sixteenth whole fleets of 200 to 300 ships arrived twice a year with cargoes which soon found buyers in Amsterdam. The Dutch ships however also took valuable goods with them as cargo subsidiary to the bulk goods they most preferred: here, too, they had access to a commodity highly prized in the east in the form of cloth from Leyden and certain other towns of Southern Holland, whose industry, after the decline of the Flemish cloth industry, was just reaching its peak; finally, western goods which until then had been tied to the Bruges centre now found their way eastwards direct from Amsterdam. The Dutch, particularly Amsterdam, shipping had a far more dangerous effect on the Hansa than did the entry of English cloth exports into the Baltic; it robbed her of the old privileged position in the west as the unchallenged middleman, and rendered hopeless her every attempt to maintain her old privileged position by means of economic measures, for instance trade barriers. Nothing therefore could be more dangerous for the Hansa than the rise of an eastwards-looking large-scale shipping enterprise in the west. The Dutch embarked on their Baltic service in alliance with Denmark against the Hansa, and in doing so signed the latter's death warrant. Amsterdam grew up into what for Baltic trade was the leading position in the west; the decline of Antwerp and the age of discoveries subsequently presented the town with new and splendid tasks to perform.

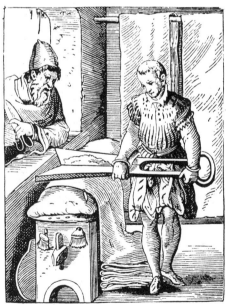

17   A Flemish clothworker
From a sixteenth-century engraving
by J. Ammam

5

LÜBECK AND
NUREMBERG

❀

Our intention up to now has been to indicate individual lines of development in the history of European towns, and to demonstrate in this way the essentials of urban development from its origins and in its actual existence. This aim was also pursued in the sketch of Flemish-Dutch urban development in the last chapter. In the process it became apparent how heterogeneous was the development of towns even within a relatively small area. Even here there is no integrated history of the town. Bruges and Ypres, Liège and Brussels, Antwerp and Amsterdam have no common denominator in their internal structure and the historical process of their destinies, not to mention the smaller towns such as those lying east of the Zuider Zee. Apart from this the face of individual towns has been transformed from the earliest times of the emergence of towns to the beginning of recent centuries. The commercial attitude of towns which once possessed the greatest economic strength became tired and narrow-minded, while other towns rose and gave an impression of vigour and youth compared with those which were trying to maintain or revive a past age of prosperity with inadequate means. Thus it becomes apparent how questionable it is to talk about 'the' medieval town as a social type of a well-defined nature, or to look for a single commercial spirit and organisation in it which, in contrast to the modern 'capitalist'-organised town, was founded on an order supported in the first place by the 'corporation' system, which guaranteed each individual townsman his daily bread and prevented the emergence of a spirit of acquisitiveness as the motive force of trade.

It is not by chance that these viewpoints were widespread in Germany itself. But the history of German towns seems most clearly to demonstrate from contemporary sources the contrast between the medieval and the modern town, in particular in the contrast between the Hanseatic and the South German towns of the sixteenth century. This contrast of quite different commercial attitudes between Southern and Northern German towns is very clearly illustrated by a late, but particularly clear testimony. Between Nuremberg and Lübeck there existed differences of opinion as to how the other town's merchants should be treated. Nuremberg allowed every foreigner in the town to do as he would; Lübeck on the other hand subjected him to all kinds of trade restrictions, prevented him from buying small quantities of goods from local retailers, forbade the alien merchant from publicly displaying his wares, and tried to force him to sell all the goods he had brought with him, even if he lost on the deal through inadequate tenders. In 1571 Lübeck suggested to the council of Nuremberg that Lübeck merchants in Nuremberg should be treated in the same way as was customary with other foreign merchants there, and that conversely Nuremberg merchants in Lübeck should be treated in the manner customary in Lübeck. This would have meant that the Nurembergers in Lübeck would have been swindled according to the principles of the so-called 'guests' laws', while the Lübeckers in Nuremberg would have been able to go about their business unhindered. It was only to be expected that the council of Nuremberg should draw the Lübeck council's attention to the absurdity of such a suggestion, remarking ironically that this was no *proportio*—neither a *proportio arithmetica* nor *geometrica*.

Such was in fact the case. Commercial thinking and practice at the time could not be made to agree between a South German and a Hanseatic town. But this was equally impossible at the same time between towns such as Antwerp and Bruges. In both cases it was less a question of the difference between a 'medieval' and a 'modern' town than the difference between a town grown old, no longer in possession of its full economic strength, and a young one with as yet untapped sources of economic energy. In other words, it is not the spirit of 'the medieval town' that speaks in the unfriendly attitude of the Hanseatic town in relation to the South German, but the spirit of a late stage in the urban development of the Hansa, very clearly distinguishable from the spirit of the same town about 300 years before.

In early times the Hansa had sailed under an entirely different flag. Freedom of trade and free commercial competition were concepts just as valid as they were for Nuremberg in the sixteenth century; it was around 1300 that the most ruthless striving for profit evidently took hold in Lübeck, the leading Hanseatic town. Then things certainly began to change. The peace of Stralsund (1370) marked both a culmination and a turning-point in the history of the Hansa. The Lübeck council, at the height of success, adopted a policy of caution whose aim was to maintain what had been won in the richest measure. Something in the nature of deliberate resignation hung over Hanseatic foreign policy from that time on. And this resignation was only too well founded. We have already seen the dangers growing from the direction of the English and Flemish coasts which threatened the Hanseatic commercial position in the west—the import of English cloth, brought about by this and by the decline of Bruges which was closely associated with it, undermining the key position of Hanseatic trade in the west. And then the Dutch Baltic shipping was a devastating invasion of the actual basis of Hanseatic economy. But bad as were the consequences of the Dutch lines for the Hanseatic towns, their unhealthy influence was far from being restricted to this: nothing weakened the inner unity of the towns more than did, in a quite different way, the Dutch traffic through the Sound. This affected both the so-called Wendic towns grouped around Hamburg and Lübeck, and the Hanseatic towns on the eastern seaboard. For the eastern Baltic towns, who now jealously reserved the selling of the goods from their hinterland for their own burghers, the cheap cargo space offered by the Dutch was not undesirable, especially since their own roadstead was not at all well developed. For the Wendic towns, which lived only from intermediate trade, Dutch competition was annihilating. Clearer and clearer and ever more public became the contrast between the eastern and western Hanseatic towns—and this at the precise moment when the Danish threat was becoming the more immediate in that the Dutch were seeking and finding their obvious allies in Denmark. It was in the face of this Dutch-Danish problem that the Hansa finally disintegrated as a political power at the beginning of the sixteenth century. The entirely different form of relationship between city and state in Germany, and that of the area of Hanseatic interest lying outside the boundaries of Germany, both of which we have already looked at, did their bit to ensure the final political decline and fall of the Hansa.

The splendid political ability and diplomatic skill demonstrated again and again in the internal and external leadership of the towns were certainly able to postpone this inevitable decline, and delay the end to an almost unbelievable degree, but they could not hold it indefinitely at bay. Evidently the decline of Hanseatic power had its internal effect too, most of all in the hardest hit Wendic towns and their headquarters, Lübeck. Political and private commercial activities in the leading Hanseatic personalities had grown far too much together for it to have been otherwise. The result was therefore a real structural change, a transformation which gave the town as commercial organisation quite a different aspect. In early Lübeck trade and its interests had ruled as absolutely as in the Flemish towns of the same time—a trade carried on by strong individuals, by their ruthless striving to exploit the splendid profit-making opportunities of the newly opened up commercial world. But now the leaders of the upper class were the more thoughtful descendants of those same bold merchants and they wished to retain the riches of a more fortunate age as far as possible in their original state, and to enjoy a life on unearned income in a society separated into castes. Of course trade remained even then the most important occupation of the merchants; but people were more careful than before, and were not very pleased, for instance, when acquisitively inclined individuals threatened the management of their colleagues' businesses. With this position directed towards the continuation and maintenance of a certain way of life, the upper

18 Merchants on the Rhine
From a woodcut of 1484

class of the fifteenth century stood fundamentally closer to the commercial outlook of the manual workers and their unions than to their own ancestors, whose unbridled creative urges had made the formation of an upper class of men of private means impossible until the end of the thirteenth century. On top of this they had to make concessions to the manual workers over the organisation of commerce if the latter were to be prevented from making dangerous experiments in systems of government, which were by no means lacking even in Lübeck. This was the basis of that conception of commerce which we shall deal with in detail as a 'closed municipal commerce'. But this change meant for the Hansa a diminishing of its former field of activity, and an exaggerated stress was laid on the commercial interests of the individual town which very soon led to a commercial policy of discrimination on the part of one Hanseatic town towards the merchants of another. The successful attempts of Riga in the fifteenth century to prevent the merchants of another Hanseatic town from going beyond Riga, thus forcing them to get goods from the Dvina only from the merchants of Riga, are a clear example of how little protectionist measures in the field of trade in favour of the individual town were consistent with the original idea of the Hanseatic commercial system. In these circumstances it was not to be wondered at that the people of the Hansa tried to make the trading activities of foreign merchants, such as those of Nuremberg, difficult in a Hanseatic town, and it was out of such tensions that grew those unpleasantnesses in the traffic between Nuremberg and Lübeck with which this chapter began.

At the time when Lübeck still subscribing to principles of free trade, Nuremberg, far inferior in commercial significance, was distinguished by ordinances directed against outsiders. But after the end of the fourteenth century—a particularly favourable one for Nuremberg—her development took a totally opposite course from that of Lübeck. From then on an upper class formerly only concerned with commercial interests, which had allowed no such thing as a workers' guild to exist, abolished all existing restrictions on foreign merchants in Nuremberg and planned a far-sighted and thoroughly rational commercial policy. In the course of the fifteenth century restrictions on length of stay were as good as suppressed, the prohibition on trading commission on foreign account was done away with, and trade association with aliens was permitted. The council did not even allow itself to be swayed in this long-term policy by the population's murmurings that foreigners were being favoured. For the ordinances favouring aliens were only a part of those measures with which the council intended to turn Nuremberg into a trading place continually visited by foreign merchants and indeed indispensable to them. The second method by which they sought to achieve this aim was by improving the quality of Nuremberg's industry, in the interest of her commerce, which dominated and controlled it, to the highest degree of quality, and thus to give Nuremberg's commerce a world-wide reputation by means of its own products. This purpose was served by the rigorous 'show' of goods produced by the industry of Nuremberg. Armour and swords, goblets and products of the metal-working industry carrying the sign of the Nuremberg exhibition were prized everywhere in Germany and elsewhere; the splendid tombstones from Peter Vischer's workshop followed the merchant who went and settled in Lübeck, Poznan and Cracow. On the other hand the council kept the small man in a good mood by seeing to it that his daily requirements of food and luxuries were not made any dearer by unnecessary middlemen. But above all, the Nuremberg metal industry would never have achieved such an importance in a town thoroughly unfavoured by Nature if trade itself had not in the most methodical way brought the raw materials to Nuremberg from a long way away. Bohemian, Saxon and Hungarian copper was procured and worked in the liquation shops of Nuremberg. In the fifteenth century copper requirements still led to the erection of liquation plants by Nuremberg entrepreneurs in Thuringia, where Mansfeld copper was worked, and the Nuremberg merchants, organised in large companies with a large capital, made the shop masters dependent on them by means of a system of advances on the copper that was to be delivered. The volume of this metal industry—we have only mentioned copper here—went far beyond the requirements of Nuremberg trade and strengthened the position of the Nuremberg merchant, particularly in the Netherlands. The very remarkable efforts on the part of the Nuremberg trader to be not only a middleman but also to monopolise the entire range of production of some of his goods, led later on to credit agreements on advances with the linen weavers' guilds of the Upper Lusatian towns, particularly Zittaus, which assured the linen from these regions for the Nuremberg merchant. Here too the Nuremberg industry had a direct advantage in the arrangements made by the merchants of its town, since a good part of this eastern linen was finished in Nuremberg dyeing-shops.

Apart from the great creative phenomenon of the creation of the Hanseatic economy from the twelfth to the fourteenth centuries nothing in the history of the German town up to 1500 can compare with the commercial wisdom and degree of organisation which were responsible for the consolidation of the position of Nuremberg in world trade from the fourteenth to the sixteenth centuries. Its merchants pushed south-east as far as Constantinople and westwards as far as Spain. Admittedly it was the Welsers of Augsburg, the largest company in the goods trade, who established a base in Lisbon and from there fitted out a highly profitable expedition to the East Indies in 1505. But apart from Lisbon, the Nuremberg merchants of the fifteenth century were to be found in all the places in Europe in which the German merchant might be interested. As suppliers of oriental goods via Italy, and of the quality goods of northern Italy itself, they were interested in Venice, Genoa, Milan and in the paper industry of Brescia to the extent to which they were able to gain and keep the north as a selling-place for these goods and for Nuremberg products. They could be found just as often at the Geneva fairs of the fifteenth century as, after the decline of Geneva, in Lyon. The Lower Rhine, with Cologne as its centre, was a goal of ever-increasing importance; Antwerp above all drew the Nuremberg merchant into its magnetic field. The East in its broadest sense, from Wrocław up to Gdansk, and far beyond this line, as far as Warsaw and Lublin, Lvov and Cracow, was the Nuremberg merchant's field of activity at this time; Austria and Hungary could not do without him. However much Augsburg may have outshone Nuremberg in the sixteenth century as the town of the great European banking business, Nuremberg remained with its goods trade, in any case in the fifteenth century, unparalleled in size and organisation.

At the time when increasing xenophobia in the Hanseatic region and elsewhere threatened to restrict the trading activities of the foreign merchant, whole groups of Nuremberg merchants settled in the most important of these towns in a way which was obviously planned, obtained civic rights, and proceeded to further the trade of the members of their families in Nuremberg to the highest degree. In the sixties and seventies of the fifteenth century—and even before and after this time—quite a large number of Nuremberg merchants settled in Lübeck, men of respected families such as the Mulichs or the Münzers who enjoyed a position of distinction in Lübeck and were particularly well regarded by the Leonhard Brotherhood. Exactly the same process was being carried out in Poznan at the same time. Wroclaw and Cracow, but above all Leipzig accepted Nurembergers, and along with them many other merchants from places in southern Germany as merchants of their towns. At the turn of the fifteenth and sixteenth centuries Nurembergers acquired positions in the east, particularly again in Leipzig, in inverse proportion to the decline of Lübeck. It was one of the most decisive achievements of Nuremberg's commercial policy that it managed to steer the central European east–west trade off its old tracks and through the new central point of Nuremberg. This was true not only of the old Hanseatic east–west route but also for Regensburg whose old lines of traffic to the west petered out at this time in the face of the new Nuremberg line. Regensburg and Lübeck, both of which in the fourteenth century far outstripped Nuremberg in commercial importance, became declining stars in the later Middle Ages. Leipzig, drawn into the eastern route from Nuremberg, now began to increase in importance, although at first still overshadowed by Nuremberg. The insecurity of the trade routes from Nuremberg south of the Erzebirge Mountains to Prague and Wroclaw, important as these towns were to the German merchant in the fourteenth century, arose out of the Hussite troubles and was partly responsible for the blossoming of Leipzig. The fact that in 1492 Kilian Auer, a Nuremberger, acting as agent for a trading company to which a Fugger of Augsburg also belonged, exchanged cloth from Mechlin and Maastricht for furs in Poznan, is only a fragment of proof of the fact that the old Hanseatic monopoly in the exchange of valuable cloth from the west for smoked goods from the east no longer existed. It was not long before Leipzig was occupying the position which once had belonged to Lübeck as the leading place in the fur trade. Direct supply of Dutch herring through the Nuremberg merchant made the south independent of the deliveries of salted or dried fish via Lübeck. From the west, the influx of Netherlands cloth to Nuremberg greatly increased in the fifteenth century; much of it, perhaps most of it, went further eastwards, while in the opposite direction Nuremberg by a clever tariff policy, was able to divert the through trade particularly of eastern wax. Southern and central Germany increasingly freed themselves from the Hanseatic carrying trade, though earlier both Frankfurt and Nuremberg had been grateful customers.

Nuremberg acceded to the first position in the goods trade of Germany around 1500. Without the strong support of Nuremberg and its merchants any trade between the rest of southern Germany and the east was almost unthinkable. The trading company of the Diesbach-Watts, which at first was based in Berne and St Gallen, the most important place after Constance for the export of linen, developed its whole eastern trade in the closest association with the eastern connections of Nuremberg. One of its founders, Peter von Watt, settled in Nuremberg to look after the eastern interests of his company, and married a Pirkheimer. He was not the only company man in Nuremberg; indigenous Nurembergers followed as partners in the company. It was these who carried on the company's business in the east. Important as was the St Gallen linen for the company, without Nuremberg metal goods its trade would have been no more noteworthy than that of the largest trading company dealing in goods in the late Middle Ages, the so-called Great Company whose headquarters were in the quiet town of Ravensburg. Everything that could be bought in Nuremberg in the way of metal goods, from raw material to the finest finished products, can be clearly demonstrated from the business books and papers of this company, since a literary monument has been erected to it by Aloys Schulte. It was certainly no

19 Nuremberg in the late fifteenth century

From Schedel, 'Weltchronik', 1493

coincidence that in the company's ledgers of 1497 the assets of its Nuremberg representative (or *Lieger*) were far and away the most important of all the representatives; they were recorded at 42,642 Rhenish guilders. The Nuremberg representative of the company was also responsible for the important town of Frankfurt. An indication of the real position of supremacy enjoyed by Nuremberg in the east was that she took diplomatic steps in Silesia on behalf of burghers of Ravensburg—obviously employees of the Great Company—who had been imprisoned. By and large Nuremberg was the eastern base of the Great Company; merchants preferred to get north-eastern goods in Nuremberg itself—a clear proof of their preference for the Nuremberg market, which made it possible for the foreign merchant to buy there so cheaply, that it was not worth his while pushing beyond Nuremberg to compete with the Nuremberg trader. It was no kind of coercion that bound the trader west of Nuremberg to the Nuremberg market, but the fruits of a free and far-sighted trade policy on the part of Nuremberg. The trading area of the Great Company was imposingly widespread. It had agents in Venice, Milan and Genoa, in Berne and Geneva, in Lyon and Avignon, in Bourg-en-Bresse and Bouc near Marseille, in Perpignan and Toulouse, in Barcelona, Saragossa and Valencia, in Tortosa, Alicante and Bilbao, in Bruges (this agency was replaced by one in Antwerp), in Vienna and Pest, as well as in Nuremberg. Nevertheless this proud organisation remained everywhere within the framework of Nuremberg trade; only in Spain may the company have been more important than Nuremberg.

The Nuremberg-South German goods trade, imposing as it was, was not fundamentally different from those trade organisations which had earlier been created in the Mediterranean, in Flanders and also in the Hanseatic region. New, strange characteristics only appear with the rapid growth of banking and the connection of trade with industrial undertakings, firstly in mining. In banking Italy, and in particular Florence and Venice took the lead; Antwerp and Augsburg followed. The 'Age of the Fuggers' began. The contrast between Lübeck and Nuremberg in the fifteenth century was not a fundamental one; but trade in Nuremberg at that time was in full bloom, while in the north the flowering was already over.

6

THE URBAN
POPULATION

❃

Since two German towns—Lübeck and Nuremberg—turn out to be organisms of such dissimilar evolution, we shall have to overcome a certain timidity if at the same time we nevertheless wish to derive answers to individual questions of urban life from the information we have for different towns. This is indispensable, however, if we are to give a general view in such a small space; and it will not be dangerous provided we compare evidence only from towns which share a similar structure, and provided we bear in mind the local and chronological differences between what is being compared, and refrain from straining comparisons and making unjustifiable generalisations.

The difference in population of medieval towns indicates the various degrees of activity and the various functions of individual towns. Not all so-called towns, not even those which may, legally, have been a town in the sense that this or that little place may have had 'urban rights' bestowed upon it by some lord, can be included in an exposition whose aim is to elucidate the essential elements that made the medieval town into one of the most important impulses in world history. Nowadays we have freed ourselves from the notion that the medieval map of Germany was dotted with about 3,000 towns, each of which had the same aim—namely, as the central point of a minute territorial economic area, to lead as self-contained a life as the old manor farm of the local seigneur had once led. By far the greater part of these 3,000 'towns'—about 2,800—had populations of less than 1,000; in other words, there is no question of their being considered as truly urban economies, least of all as self-contained ones, because there was really no possibility that within these tiny little populations there would be room enough for all the trades necessary to the self-sufficiency of a town, however modest. A further 150 'towns', roughly speaking, also very modest even by medieval standards, had populations of between 1,000 and 2,000. Only the remaining ones, about fifty of them, were towns of any real importance within the German economy, over half of which, with populations of less than 10,000, formed the German medium-sized towns. Finally there was a group of about fifteen large German towns whose populations were in excess of 10,000. Cologne was the largest with more than 30,000 inhabitants; the second largest was Lübeck with no more than 25,000 around 1400. Apart from these only Strasbourg, Nuremberg, Gdansk and perhaps Ulm would have reached and exceeded 20,000 in the fifteenth century. Towns of the rank of Frankfurt am Main, Wroclaw, Zürich and Augsburg grew from 10,000 to 18,000 in the course of the fifteenth century; in 1493 the population of Erfurt amounted to about 18,500. If the population of Leipzig is calculated at around 4,000 in 1474, then this is the clearest possible indication of the huge increase which this town experienced since then, mainly as an ancillary member of the Nuremberg trading system.

Similar conditions obtained in the northern European towns outside Germany. Of English towns only London had more than 10,000 inhabitants, and this certainly by a considerable amount; it already had 30–40,000 in the fourteenth century. An even higher incidence of population in a capital is certainly known to have obtained in Paris. This town, as the royal residence, as an episcopal see and as the seat of the famous university, exercised at the height of the Middle Ages a power of attraction such as did no other town north of the Alps. Among the Flemish towns Bruges appears, at least at the time of its greatest prosperity, to have had the largest population within its walls. It is somewhat surprising that Ypres had only a little more than 10,000 inhabitants; admittedly this was in 1412, when the Flemish weaving towns were already in decline and the weavers' suburbs depopulated. Ypres, but also particularly Ghent would have had far greater numbers in the fourteenth century. Figures far in excess of the German towns were to be found particularly in Italy. Florence is supposed to have had 100,000 inhabitants around 1340; its decline from that time on is well known. Milan is said to have had 85,000 inhabitants towards the end of the fifteenth century. In the sixteenth century the respective populations of Venice, Naples and Palermo are all believed to have exceeded 100,000.

But nothing would be more mistaken than to underestimate a medieval German town of 20,000 people in terms of the function that it fulfilled in the Middle Ages simply because in modern times a town of this size is not usually very important. Within the framework of the whole, a German town of around that number of inhabitants in 1400 fulfilled a political, economic and cultural function of which many a present-day town of several hundred thousands would be envious. Even if one evaluates Aeneas Sylvius Piccolomini's account of German towns, particularly Cologne, Strasbourg and Nuremberg, in the middle of the fifteenth century as conscious exaggeration—nevertheless he was not the only foreigner to emphasise the outstanding importance of German towns; Cologne, particularly, was a match for any other town of Europe. Machiavelli even saw in the German town the heart of Germany's strength.

Certainly this urban population was subject to a terrible danger which could reduce its numbers very considerably. This was the scourge of the plague—the Black Death—which particularly in the middle of the fourteenth century held its slow but ineluctable victory procession throughout the countries of Europe, of which the best propagators were the flagellants, driving the terrible disease before them. The towns, with their populations squeezed within their walls, had the largest sacrifices to make. It is assumed that the population of Florence was reduced by a third in the terrible mass death of 1348. It was the lowest classes, the weavers, who were the most thoroughly depleted; a renewed outbreak of the plague hit the town in 1374. Western Europe was no less badly hit; England is thought to have lost up to half her population. Germany, too, hit by the first wave of the plague in 1349–50, suffered greatly. According to an entry in the citizens' book of Bremen, 6,966 known and named persons were carried off by it in the town.

The medieval town knew better how to defend itself against famine than against the plague. In this connection a careful policy of stock-piling on the part of the town council served as a precaution against times of corn shortage and war; and above all they saw to it that stocks of food stored either by the town or privately under municipal control did not perish. In cases of regional corn shortage in a region a foreign trade correspondingly intervened. The Flemish towns were dependent on regular corn imports from the Baltic as early as the thirteenth century; inland towns such as Görlitz were regularly supplied with corn from the east.

A continual and heavy restriction on increase in population was the unfavourable formation of the natural class structure in the urban population. Certainly many children were born. But the infant mortality rate was perhaps even more remarkable than the number of births. Of the twenty-one children of Konrad Paumgartner, a Nuremberg councillor and merchant who died in 1464, only five sons continued the line and four daughters married. Nevertheless shortly before his death Konrad Paumgartner saw seventy-four grandchildren and forty great-grandchildren growing up around him. The Rorach family of Frankfurt saw sixty-five children come into the world between the end of the fourteenth and the end of the sixteenth centuries who lived; but only eighteen of them outlived their fathers, and only twelve married! High infant mortality rates were certainly common to both the town and the countryside; but in the towns there was the additional ominous problem of the third or fourth generation, particularly in the most distinguished families. One can observe again and again how the grandchildren of economically outstanding fathers grew weak in business sense, preferring to live on fixed investments and died without leaving an heir. One can see just as frequently a branch of an old merchant family living an aristocratic-lord-of-the-manor life in the country and blossoming for generations, long after the original family in the town had died out. People in the towns were quite well aware of this disastrous process. When in 1548 a senior minister in Rostock dedicated a work to the Lübeck patrician Kinrich Castorp he wrote in the dedication:

> Among all the families of Lübeck there are not three or four in which there is a living member of the fourth generation. It makes you angry, said Moses, that we thus perish, and raging that we must thus disappear. May the Lord promise and give to you, the fourth successor of your house, and to your father's and your mother's families everything which is good through Christ, temporally and eternally.

In spite of these good wishes however the house of Castorp died out with the man of the dedication. It was a consequence of this unfavourable condition for natural succession that the towns so encouraged the move from the country to the towns—we may remember the saying, 'Town air brings freedom'—an encouragement strongly opposed by the lords of the countryside.

Even the ratio of the sexes was not a happy one. Notwithstanding the fact that an unusually high proportion of women died in childbirth, they were still more numerous than men in the urban population. In towns like Nuremberg, Basle and Rostock in the fifteenth century, for every 1,000 men there were respectively 1,207, 1,246 and 1,295 women. The greater dangers run by the armed merchants of the town, their frequently immoderate way of life, perhaps also their higher mortality in epidemics have been seen as the causes of this unequal proportion of the sexes by K. Bücher. In the light of this it is understandable that the laws of Lübeck allowed the same legal position to women in their business affairs as it did to men as early as the thirteenth century; and indeed how it came about that women could be members of workers' guilds. In far and away the largest proportion of such cases it was a question of widows; many a young journeyman was only able to become master in his trade by marrying his mistress. Such marriages were the breeding-ground for the much disparaged 'shrew', a problem which has often been illustrated by medieval art with extreme bluntness. The frequent marriages of widows diminished for many unmarried women their chances of marriage, already slight enough on account of the preponderance of women.

There was also the fact that in a town like Lübeck at least three or four hundred men could not be considered for marriage on account of their being secular priests or regular clergy. In these circumstances nunneries became social institutions of great importance. Again and again in medieval merchant's wills one meets with stipulations that if the young growing daughters of the testator do not succeed in finding a husband they must buy their way into a nunnery with a certain sum of money. Marriage or the veil was the only solution in the most distinguished families. The upper class of Lübeck considered not only the St John's Nunnery of Lübeck but a whole series of nunneries in Mecklenburg and Holstein, Rehna, Neukloster, Zarrentin and Preetz among them— as places where their unmarried daughters would be looked after, and endowed them richly with earthly goods. The *Klosterfahrt,* or ceremony of admission, was celebrated with great pomp; no greater proof of this fact is needed than the frequent attempts to limit the amounts spent even here. For women of lower class, hospitals offered a refuge and a living. Even more important, and highly characteristic of town life in the fourteenth and fifteenth centuries, were the Beguine houses, which looked after the unmarried women of the middle and lower strata of the population. There is without doubt a connection between the proponderance of women and the distribution of Beguine houses, which were most patronised in the Netherlands, but which were to be seen in German towns everywhere, most numerous in the Rhenish towns and least so in the colonial regions. The inmates of a convent—often less than ten and never more than fifty—led a communal life, but the life of a lay community and not the *vita religiosa* of the nuns. Between 1250 and 1350 about 100 Beguine houses, which together had room for at least 1,000 women, are said to have been founded in Cologne. The Beguine houses in Strasbourg had room for about 600 sisters. In Lübeck there were only five convents with about 100 sisters; but on the whole there was room here for 600 women in institutions which had come into being for single women. But as much as reasons of care and attention were emphasised as being responsible for the large number of

20 London in the fifteenth century, looking from the
Tower to London Bridge
British Museum, Royal MS. 16 F. 2, f. 73a

21   The Scheldt Gate at Antwerp in 1520
From a pen drawing by Albrecht Dürer

22   A Nuremberg tourney, 1561
Detail from a painting by J. Ammam

Beguine convents, nevertheless, as places in which a strongly religious life was led, they had great importance in the development of medieval piety. Their societies were also full of the search for Christian perfection which brought convents here and there into conflict with the official church authorities. In most cases, however, these sisters fitted into the life of the church and town without difficulty, living off the income of the endowments and also performing works of various kinds. On the other hand it did occur later on that the rich foundations of the convents led to an unhealthy idleness amongst the inmates, which occasionally brought them into disrepute.

The Jews, who led a special existence by religion and by law deserve a special note. It was not as though there were Jews in every town; the chronicler remarks of Lübeck—a town which was highly self-conscious as a place of commerce: 'There are no Jews in Lübeck; there is no need for them either.' He was right; for even without Jews such things as money-lending and usury, mortgages and foreclosures were everyday things in Lübeck; in the same way Florentine banks were created by Italian entrepreneurs, and Italian, Hanseatic and English merchants of the fourteenth century carried on money businesses of considerable size for the English crown. The good and bad results of a commercial enterprise directed towards personal gain also affected towns which had nothing whatever to do with Jews. All this in spite of ecclesiastical prohibition of usury—a prohibition which, like so many, is to be taken rather as evidence that in fact things happened quite differently from the way in which the prohibitors, in this case the ecclesiastical moral theorists, supposed and demanded. Quite unabashed, the council of Constance forbade its townsmen to take more than eleven per cent on the money they lent. Moreover, the behaviour of the church itself was most strangely at variance with the demands of its moral theoreticians. On the other hand it is wrong to imagine that the Jews were restricted to money-lending. Like the Christians, they, too, combined trade in goods with money-lending—in the early centuries they were pioneers in foreign trade. Certainly in the later Middle Ages they concentrated on money-changing and banking, and particularly pawnbroking. Lords of the manor, knights and towns found themselves among the debtors of Jewish money-lenders; but also did a whole lot of small people—cobblers, tailors and sadlers. If the hatred of Jews in many towns reached special intensity in the fourteenth century, then this is connected with the fact that the small people, too, saw in them the burdensome, and certainly also frequently usurious creditor. To this, moreover, was added the religious contrast which divided Jews from Christians far more sharply than did the economic contrast, which in any case was to some extent artificially engendered by the church.

The first wave of persecution of the Jews in Western Europe was bound up with the crusading atmosphere, the second with the advance of the Black Death in the fourteenth century. It was at the beginning of 1348, when the plague was raging in a town of Provence, that in May of that year the first Jews were burnt. From there the rumour that the Jews had poisoned the wells of the town buzzed through the land, even throughout South, West and Central Germany. In most cases the Jews had already met their fate before the plague even hit the town, as in Strasbourg, where the chronicler confesses that money was the sole reason for the killing of the Jews. If they had been poor and the lords had not been indebted to them, they would not have been burnt. If the picture given of the burning of the Jews in Strasbourg is correct—apart from the certainly exaggerated total given of Jews burnt (2,000)—then it becomes clear that religious hate was stronger than racial antipathy. If a Strasbourg Jew consented to be baptised he stayed alive; many small children are said to have been taken from the burning pyre and baptised against their parents' wishes. Frederick I's Jews' Charter of 1157 had already forbidden the baptism of secretly stolen Jewish children. Subsequent rulers were not able to withstand the temptation to exploit their rights of protection of the Jews ruthlessly for their own enrichment. However it would be wrong to assume that persecution of the Jews was the rule; decades of peace and lawfulness were suddenly interrupted by catastrophes. In the large towns it was in fact the circles of council and merchant families which energetically protected the Jews at least from arrest without trial, mob law and the like in the interests of law and order within the town until far into the fourteenth century. The worsening of the Jews' position in the towns is reflected also in the circumstances of their living quarters and the property they owned. The real obligation to live in a spatially enclosed Jewish settlement within the town, which was locked up at night—the ghetto—only set in towards the end of the thirteenth century. After the persecution of the Jews in the fourteenth century, remote streets and corners were set apart for them.

23 Burning of the Jews of Cologne
From a woodcut of 1493

7

PATRICIATE AND
WORKING CLASS

❀

It is when we come to consider the question of occupations that we can see how the main problems connected with the history of medieval town populations lead us to consider trade and manual labour. As varied as were the individual urban developments we have dealt with up to now, they were identical on one count—the fact that in the life of the larger medieval town the most important thing was trade. It was only logical that the long-distance traders of the developing patriciate, the urban upper class, should turn out to be the real core of this new social formation—a class of traders in possession of the most valuable property of the town, and which, in the case of the most valuable goods such as Flemish cloth, could also keep for itself the business of cutting up the cloth into smaller pieces. This was, however, only one of many functions, and by no means even a principal one, which would have meant that those concerned could have been called 'small traders'. One must also reckon with the large number of employees who were early in evidence; there was no need for the patrician himself to be continually present in the garment shop with yardstick and shears. But, as with all manifestations of medieval life in commerce, government and society, when considering the history of this upper class, we must take particular account of differences in time and place. We are after all dealing with developments first noticeable for instance in the Rhenish towns in the eleventh century, and easily span the period of time we are concerned with here. In one and the same town there could be a world of difference between the early structure, commercial activity and function of that part of the population which crystallised into the upper class and what they became in later centuries. What really characterised the upper class above all, was the fact that the families welded together within it controlled most of the important offices in the town, that is, the positions of town councillor and mayor. As long as the leading families occupied the council they effectively ruled the town. Later on, where the unions were continually successful in overthrowing the aristocratic council, or where the rulers' power destroyed autonomy, there was only room for a class of 'notables'. But these were not by any means families who had belonged for centuries to the upper class. The short life-span of most urban families would have prevented that. But in any case the intrinsic connection between trade and the upper class was unfavourable to any exclusiveness on the part of families belonging to this class.

We have already noticed how in Lübeck a complete reshuffle of those families eligible for the council took place at the end of the thirteenth century; and this precisely because at a time of commercial boom those people connected with the new trade largely replaced the descendants of the old upper class of entrepreneurs by means of their unprecedented wealth. It was the same with Vienna. Such reshuffles were repeated within the circles of upper-class families wherever commercial conditions remained favourable. In Wroclaw in the fifteenth century, the recent immigrants forced an entry into the council by means of their commercial sense, and though they could not break into the social world of the resident upper class, the latter soon lost its political leadership in the town. On the other hand, in Nuremberg—the classical patrician town of the late Middle Ages—not only did the upper class retain the connection with trade which it inherited from its previous members, but it continued to absorb new and competent merchants into its ranks. Because at that time the leading families of Nuremberg, in company with merchants of the second-highest class of notables, took such a far-sighted part in the new forms of trade with metals, Nuremberg was able to maintain and extend its position of leadership in the German economy well into modern times. Conversely Lübeck's political and commercial development led to the damping of commercial ardour, and thus made possible the formation of a class of people living off unearned income which was only able to maintain itself in a position of complete social distinction in a decadent or stagnant economy. Here, where the upper class had formed itself into the 'Circle' in 1379, closing itself off from the outside world, tensions had already begun to arise towards the end of the fourteenth century between the upper class and individual, clever foreign-traders who were excluded from entry into the upper class. Such a one was Hinrich Paternoster-maker, the son of a successful trader and himself a trader over great distances, as far as Berne for example, who in 1384 placed himself at the head of an uprising directed against the council and those whom he described as the capitalists of the Circle, and who lost his life and possessions in so doing. But in the long run the foreign-trading upper class of Nuremberg knew better how to defend its supremacy *vis-à-vis* the workers than did the capitalists of Lübeck, who for political reasons made concessions to the unions in the field of commerce which jeopardised the commercial character of the town.

The position of the upper class in relation to the nobility was no more uniform. At first, in colonial towns such as Lübeck and Vienna, the upper stratum of merchants still felt itself inherently superior to the ruler's officials. This is clearly seen in the marriage laws. For the daughter of a Viennese merchant, marriage to a *miles*, a knight, meant loss of freedom and wealth. In Lübeck, too, a merchant's daughter in such a case could only take with her what she had on—a condition which suggests at least that such marriages were undesirable to the upper middle class. It is significant however that this condition disappeared in Lübeck as early as the thirteenth century, and that Rudolf of Hapsburg's law for Vienna expressly proclaims the equality of birth of upper-class families and knights. Thus it remained in the first part of the fourteenth century. Marriages between knights and daughters of the upper middle class, entry of members of distinguished merchant families into the Teutonic Order, the high number of sons from merchant families who became bishops and members of cathedral chapters, particularly in the colonial east, the frequent exchange of individuals between country nobility and the patriciate into feudal classes and court officialdom—all these are clear indications of how blurred were the divisions at that time between the upper middle class and the knightly nobility. From the late fourteenth century the relationship of the upper middle class to the nobility shifted, as the latter continued to decline in military importance, but at the same time its self-consciousness of itself as a class increased. The nobility began to recognise the urban patriciate as members of an admittedly higher rank, but one nevertheless which was still properly townsman, and thus fundamentally lower-born. With remarkable arrogance it maintained that the only difference between the townsman and the peasants was that the former were ensconced within the city wall. The actual circumstances were certainly very little affected by evaluations of such a nature; if we had only portraits of the urban upper class of around 1500 to go by—such as that of Claus Stalburg from Frankfurt or the exquisite portraits of Nuremberg notables by Albrecht Dürer—they would be sufficient indication that we are dealing here with men who were in positions of eminence in the life of their time, respected and valued according to standards quite different from those of a whimsical class arrogance. It was a direct product of these tendencies that towards the end of the fifteenth century the nobles' associations of South Germany expressly denied the right of the urban patriciate to participate in tournaments. Far more serious was the dispute about the patriciate's right to occupy high ecclesiastical office, for which a particular social quality was demanded; it was mainly a question of cathedral chapters and collegiate churches, but also nobles' monasteries. Because of this the patriciate was no longer able to look after many members of its families in a manner befitting their status.

The intra-urban development of the upper class is also partly responsible for the disdainful manner in which its members were treated by the lesser nobility towards the end of the fifteenth century. Patrician fellowships had been thriving since the fourteenth century, along with their exclusive drinking-houses and men's clubs such as the *Stubengesellschaft* in Ulm, the drinking-house *Zum Sünfzen* in Lindau, *Zur Katze* in Constance, the *Zum Esel* club in Ravensburg (made famous by the membership of the partners in the Great Ravensburg Company), the *Zirkelgesellschaft* in Lübeck, the St George's Brotherhood in Gdansk which held its meetings in the *Artushof*, and the society of *Schwarzhäupter* in Riga. Subsequently the descendants of successful merchants began to lend tone to these societies; the possession of urban property, later of rural estates, and eventually the possession of areas of legal jurisdiction and castles appeared more important than application to commerce which had been the foundation of the whole thing; then one can observe again and again how the patriciate became alienated from municipal life and municipal solidity. The new goal to be striven after became the alien, knightly-noble way of life. It was the tragedy of the German merchant class that it was unable in the late Middle Ages to maintain and live up to its own self-sufficient, exacting ideal of society. The more zealously they affected externals—coats of arms, seals and so forth—the more scorn and rejection was poured on them by the nobility. Any connection with trade, and living in the town, were proclaimed to be irreconcilable with nobility in the late Middle Ages; even royal privileges accorded to individual patriciates like that accorded to the patriciate of Ulm in 1552, only came later, and had very little effect on this. The scorn remained. Songs like this were sung about the patrician who affected nobility—

> His seal is polished, very great,
> And of a formidable weight;
> His rank comes, not from family,
> But India across the sea;
> Cash for the way of life he apes
> Is drawn from negro boys, and grapes.

Members of the urban patriciate who thought something of themselves did not always have an easy time from the arrogance of the nobility. When in 1468 the knight Bilgerin von Reischach sent a condescending letter to Hans Besserer, a merchant of Ravensburg and partner in the Great Company, who was born into one of the exclusive upper-class families of Ulm, Hans Besserer paid him back in his own coin. He couched his letter in the same terms, using the familiar form of address which the knight had used to him. A heated exchange of letters ensued about respective social positions. The knight cared nothing for the patriciate. He himself however sprang from 'noble people, knights and esquires', whereas Hans Besserer sprang only from 'merchants and trades-men'. One could not set a hood on a raven and call it a falcon! Scornfully he advised his burgher opponent not to bother about justifying his origins, but rather to go off to his drinking-house and there investigate how pepper and other goods came from Alexan-dria and Barcelona to Venice, and how the trade was in fustian!

The internal resistance offered to the demands of the nobility in its own town by the urban patriciate, which set great store by being treated and honoured as *Junker* (squires), became weaker and weaker. Many a member of rich patrician families in the smaller south-west German towns moved as early as the fifteenth century into a castle probably built at great cost. The family arms were, wherever possible, 'improved' in the knightly manner, and identity as a merchant was renounced for ever. Then they were graciously accepted into knightly society. Such a process, frequently repeated, meant a serious loss to burgherhood and burgher pride, and for the urban economy a considerable withdrawal of capital. It is easy to believe the Diesbach family chronicle when it says that the trading capital of Loy von Diesbach in Berne was 'somewhat lessened and weakened' because he indulged in the luxury of horses and mules, kept a master and twenty-five hounds, and the necessary falcon 'together with other valuable things', and dis-played as little interest in his father's business as his brothers did. It also happened that the nobility which sprang from merchant families came into sharp conflict with the town where they had won their riches. The crassest of these was perhaps Hans Paum-garten's relationship with Augsburg; in 1543 he could style himself, by virtue of imperial grant, Frieherr von Paumgarten zu Paum-garten, Konzenberg, Hohenschwangau und Erbach, and his estates and castles gave rise to admiration and envy even on the part of the princes, but he worked against his home town in a not very pleasant way and with means which were condemned by the papal curia. What he had acquired soon disappeared amongst his heirs. The shining example for the Paumgartens were the Fuggers. Their splendid policy of acquisition of land and people went back to that Jakob Fugger who deserved to be called 'the Rich'—and not only on account of his external wealth. Much of what had been acquired in mining enterprises and banking was invested, and withdrawn from the vicissitudes of trade. The Fugger princes outlived by centuries the decline of the merchant enterprises which bore their name.

In these circumstances courtly and noble viewpoints in all matters of external culture exercised a strong influence. Konrad Celtis, the 'arch-humanist', reproached the princes for having spread foreign luxury in clothes, and thus set a bad example. He said, however, that the Nuremberg council and the remaining patricians and notables had stood aloof from the fashion of luxury. The extent to which in fact Nuremberg trade was involved in the buying and selling of luxury goods is quite clearly shown by the buying-book kept by the Nuremberg merchant Paul Mulich at the Frankfurt Lent fair of 1495. From Lübeck, together with his brother Matthias he furnished the Scandinavian and North German courts with a large quantity of the most varied Italian silk and velvet materials, along with large quantities of pearls and other highly valuable and often bizarre trinkets. Again, all that is needed is a glance at the inventories of rich burghers such as the Frankfurt patrician Claus Stalburg the Rich to see what a wealth of luxury clothing, jewels and goblets was to be found in upper-class houses. A Lübeck patrician of around 1500, councillor Heinrich Kerckring, ordered from his Circle-brother Matthias Mulich in Nuremberg some white Italian velvet for his wife, and red for himself. When the velvet arrived in Lübeck, the white turned out to be so good that the wife had no further cause for complaint. But the red velvet destined for the councillor's own jacket pleased him in quality but not in colour, so he had new stuff delivered, again from Nuremberg. Sartorial luxury took on grotesque forms; the fashions began to change frequently, and patrician and noble families sometimes came to grief over them. Luxury was even made to serve the different social grades by firmly established rules. Obviously this was also a point of friction between nobility and patriciate; but in the town itself the upper class insisted upon its own particular grade of luxury in its dress and other matters, even to fixing the number of women who might visit a woman in childbirth, or the number of guests who could be asked to a wedding. The enormous number of grades of luxury displayed by the towns in the fifteenth century only goes to show however that it was impossible for regulations to prevail against dispositions which delighted in being one-up on the next man in external appearance, at whatever cost. As experienced a man as the Lübeck mayor Heinrich Brömbse was well aware of this when in the 1470's he commented that one such order of luxury in the town of Lübeck 'was scarcely observed'. But in those cases where orders of luxury were taken seriously, as in Wroclaw, there was a good deal of ill-will. As early as 1368—it was only after the terror of the Black Death that luxury in dress really came in—two burghers renounced their civic rights on the same day because their wives were forbidden to wear certain clothes!

From the class-determined regulations on luxury in the last centuries of the Middle Ages to the finer needs of the patrician's spirit there was a scarcely noticeable transition. Luxury itself, insofar as it was the product of a personal feeling for style and had a thoroughly serious basis, frequently led to the making of collections—for example of antique gems, highly esteemed and used as seals by distinguished merchants of Cologne in the fifteenth century, or of *objets d'art* such as ornaments and silver goblets. The desire for luxury in the living quarters of the patriciate also at least gave an opportunity for particular architectural achievements. We may remember the palaces of the Italian urban families of the late Middle Ages. In Northern Europe the stone houses of the patriciate go back to the time of the early Gothic, and even late Romanesque styles. In cases such as the so-called *Hôtel St Livier* in Metz, and the proud 'battle towers' in Regensburg, the outer form was dictated less by military considerations than by the desire to underline their social significance. The colonial German towns also stressed the social differences among their inhabitants in the architectural differences in residential buildings right from the start. The

Romanesque gable on what is now the *Löwenapotheke* in Lübeck is a last witness to the way of life of those old Lübeck families which went back to the time of the town's foundation. In this case it was the Stalbuks who built themselves a proud stone corner house in the thirteenth century.

The late Gothic patrician house of southern Germany was particularly ingenious in the way in which the inner courtyard was formed by surrounding it with open galleries. The façades were frequently decorated with balconies which as *Chörlein* (little choirs) could form the entrance to a private chapel. The North German brick-built house had no such projections, and thus the gable became the more artistically developed. In any case, the tastefully furnished patrician houses in Nuremberg in the fifteenth century made such a good impression on Piccolomini that he felt that princes must envy the inhabitants of such houses. The broad façades of the Swiss patricians' houses in Lucerne and Basle gave Hans Holbein the Younger a welcome field of activity for his masterly decorative talents.

The internal life of the house also brought the patrician continually in contact with art and its products. The rich silver cutlery bore the coat of arms of its owner, or his wife, as early as the fourteenth century. Since every distinguished burgher had a seal, or even several of different sizes, painters of miniatures splendidly developed this field of activity by producing them, often out of silver; here, too, the artistic treatment of the coat of arms was important. When the patrician merchant was travelling he liked to take with him a small travelling altar which in the case of that belonging to the Lübeck councillor and Circle member Heinrich Kerckring had the knee-cast of the owner and his wife mounted on it, decorated with the coat of arms of both families. The close interweaving of personal and ecclesiastical life led to an uncommonly strong and permanent impression of patrician life and thought on the churches themselves. The well-known patrician societies had their own chapel in one of the churches of their town, on whose furnishings and fittings no expense was spared. The Lübeck Circle stipulated as a special privilege that the arms of their members who died should be hung up in their chapel.

Merchant corporations set no less store by ecclesiastical representation—characteristic examples are the *Bergenfahrer* altar and
the pews of the *Bergenfahrer* and *Schonenfahrer* in St Mary's Church,
Lübeck; we may particularly remember the rosary picture of
Dürer commissioned by German merchants in Venice who are
clearly discernible in the background. A distinguished trading
company like the Great Ravensburg spent a good deal of money
on the building and maintenance of a special company chapel; it is
not known how far anxiety was responsible for this—the need to
buy off secret sins of business, unjustifiable riches—a motive testified
to by many a medieval merchant's will. The strongest impression
however has been left by individual patrician families in the care
they lavished on their departed in the churches. To have founded
a special chapel, or at least a special altar in one of the main churches
of the town was almost a matter of course. This custom had the
further advantage that the founder's right to name the priest he
wanted for services in the chapel, allowed him to look after the
interests of close, or even of distant members of his family who had
chosen the church as their profession. For the same reason the
possibility of installing sons who had taken the cloth in the cathedral chapter of the town, from where they could make their way
to the bishopric, also had a great economic significance for the
families. A large number of the most costly medieval altars were
the gifts of individual patricians. Such a one is the moving Greverade
altar of Hans Memling, whose donor exchanged the garb of a merchant for that of a priest. Since the most important people to commission altars were to be found in the largest trading towns, among
the patriciate and the wholesale traders and also in the town
council and corporations dominated by these people—patrician
societies, brotherhoods and merchants' associations—it is easy to
see how towns like Nuremberg, Cologne, Hamburg or Lübeck
held a particular attraction for artists; and further, that these
places produced altars for export. Lübeck art followed in the tracks
of Lübeck trade as far as Scandinavia and the Baltic; altars from
Nuremberg are to be found in Zwickau, Wroclaw and Cracow. It
was general custom to decorate whole chapels with motifs connected with their merchant founders. A typical example was the

church of St Maria im Kapitol in Cologne, which had two splendidly
decorated fifteenth-century chapels, one donated by the Cologne
merchant Johann Hardenrait, who was deeply involved in trade
with England and Flanders, and the other by the lawyer and
Mayor of Cologne Johann Hirtz. Altar pictures gave a welcome
opportunity for including the portrait of their donor, his wife and
even his whole family; the devotional picture of the family of
Meyer, the Mayor of Basle, by Holbein can be said to be the mature
fulfilment of this art of portraiture that was subject to a higher,
religious idea. Within it the humble, religious disposition and the
need for personal and social distinction are inextricably bound up
together.

Death, and the desire to give the individual member of the
family, and particularly its head, a permanent memorial which
should honour not only himself but also the family as a whole, was
the occasion of further artistic creation. In the fourteenth and fifteenth centuries this took the form, particularly in the Hanseatic
region, of engraved tombstones of brass, in which greater stress
was laid on a rich and imposing treatment of the garments and
accessories than on a personal likeness—the fact that they were
imported from Flanders made this impossible in any case. Tombstones, first of all with the dead person's figure cut into the stone,
and later with a life-sized representation, came increasingly into
fashion with the urban upper class from the beginning of the fourteenth century. Such a one is that of Johann von Holtzhausen and
his wife in Frankfurt cathedral. In this connection, too, along with
the form of the departed, the coat of arms also suggested possibilities for a worthy memorial. The tombstone of the great but
unlucky Mayor of Rothenburg in the first half of the fifteenth
century, Heinrich Toppler, shows his coat of arms extremely large
in relation to the whole. The coat of arms is also prominently displayed in the bronze tombstones from Peter Vischer's workshop,
as for example that in St Mary's church, Lübeck, of the Lübeck
merchant, Godard Wigerinck who had lively trade connections
with Nuremberg and Augsburg. This had no less than five coats of
arms—his own in the middle and in the four corners those of his
four wives. The rest of the work on this stone—a lion fighting with

a dog over a ball, a dragon-woman throwing herself on to another fabulous figure with the torso of a man—strikes a note of coarse humour in the middle of all this heraldic dignity, allowing us to infer that the man's married life had not exactly been a harmonious one. From the middle of the fifteenth century onwards portraiture escaped from subjection to ecclesiastical purposes even in South German art, as at this time in Northern Italy portraiture had long since become one of the mainstreams of art. The portrait emerged as a purely secular end in itself. It is very significant in this connection that the people who commissioned these portraits much more frequently belonged to the urban patriciate and the merchants than to the nobility or the clergy. It was the upper middle class which made the greatest use of the new possibilities offered by the development of a technically and above all conceptually advanced form of art, and it is thus not surprising that it should have played the major role in the secularisation of culture. In the fifteenth century there appeared portraits of leading merchants, such as those of the Tuchers and Imhofs of Nuremberg, Johann von Melem of Frankfurt and Johann Ketzler of Nuremberg. Then came the first of Albrecht Dürer's great burgher portraits, and at the beginning of the sixteenth century his splendid portrayals of Nuremberg patricians such as Jakob Muffel and Willibald Pirkheimer. Mention may also be made of the famous picture by Holbein the Younger of the German merchant Georg Gisze from the Hanseatic *Stahlhof* in London, painted in 1532.

This picture shows the merchant in his counting house. He is in the act of closing a letter; business correspondence is stuck on the wall behind bars. One of the merchant's account books is on the table, another up on the shelf. It is as though in this late picture we are to be made aware of the foundations of this enormous upsurge of the burghers' encroachment on the old church monopoly of education, so that young men from the burgher-merchant upper class should be brought up on writing and also on Latin. By a trick of fate, several wax tablets which had been used for practice in a writing school have been preserved from fourteenth century Lübeck. Among them are drafts for business correspondence. The transformation of merchant business under the influence of the new literacy would not have been so permanently effective had not also calculations and the art of using the abacus been energetically studied. In Italian towns at the beginning of the fourteenth century there existed educational books on calculation just as much as more general handbooks on business affairs. Here too, as in the teaching of writing and Latin, the commercial purpose stands clearly in the foreground—exercises were set, for instance, which were concerned with Florentine merchants buying wool in Genoa and cloth in Pisa, and the problem was to work out the selling price of these goods in Florence, taking into consideration the differences in currency, weights and measures.

But advances in education by no means benefited the whole of the urban population; to begin with it was only the merchant upper class that benefited. Two documents exist relating to the setting up of deposits in Lübeck in the same year, 1376. One originates with a merchant, the other with a craftsman. The merchant depositor empowered the guardian of the deposit to pay out to a third party, by means of a document drawn up by himself; on the other hand the wool-weaver as depositor sent a secret sign to the guardian, previously agreed upon, and probably a tally-stick, whereupon the latter paid out a sum of money, minute by comparison to the merchant's. The tally-stick was used by Lübeck craftsmen in their payments up to the end of the fifteenth century. Thus the social contrast between merchant and manual worker was made only sharper by an educational contrast which was noticeable every day.

Two further elements were of the highest importance in the education of a merchant—practice and travel. Venice was the high school for many sons of South German merchants; here in the *Fondaco dei Tedeschi*, the German merchant foundation, they could acquire knowledge of the trade in goods and the Italian practice of book-keeping. Many a boy from merchant circles could not wait to get away, like Matthäus Schwarz from Augsburg who could endure neither the parson who was instructing him at Haidenheim nor the Latin school in Augsburg, for he 'depended solely on his common sense abroad'. At the age of only seventeen he went to Italy, first to Milan and then to Genoa and finally Venice. Three

24   Georg Gisze, a Hanseatic merchant in London

From the portrait by Hans Holbein, 1532

25 Jakob Fugger, 1459–1523
From the Portrait by Albrecht Dürer, 1520

26 Jakob Fugger with his
chief clerk, Matthew Swartz
From a contemporary painting

years later he was book-keeper at the Fugger central office in Augsburg and he subsequently published a treatise on book-keeping based on his practical knowledge of business management in the Fugger branch in Venice. The young Hanseatic merchant learned at the Hanseatic settlements abroad—in Bruges, London, Bergen, Novgorod; he also had to lend an energetic hand in the *Vitten*, that is, the pieces of land under the care and government of the Hansa where the herring catches were taken in. In Flanders young Hanseatic merchants met with colleagues from South Germany who were sent there as well as to Italy and Spain to prove their suitability for employment in high positions, for example in the Great Ravensburg Company. 'Whoever promises well goes on to great things; but whoever does not wish to is allowed to remain a donkey', runs a communication directed to the French and Spanish agents of the company in 1478. It would be better for the 'young people' if they spent their free time in the office, calculating and reading letters instead of walking around the town. What the young people had most need of being warned against was the tendency to become extravagant and haughty. The young merchants could get around in the world to an astonishing degree. The grandfather of the Circle member Dietrich Hupe who died in Lübeck in 1498 was first sent, presumably from Dortmund, to a merchant friend in Cracow to get some experience. From there he went to Armenia and further into Tartary. This was certainly rather unusual; but it was quite normal to send one's sons, who were destined to become merchants in Germany and Italy, abroad to gain experience and to learn languages, as did Klaus von Diesbach in Berne at the beginning of the fifteenth century. Pilgrimages to Spain, Rome or even Jerusalem also helped to broaden the commercial horizon of the pilgrim, if he did not prefer to pay a man to do the pilgrimage for him.

Very soon sons of merchant families also devoted themselves to secular learning. The series of German burghers' sons studying at Bologna, and then at other Italian universities continues throughout the whole of the Middle Ages. At the end of the thirteenth century, in 1299, two members of the families on the Lübeck council, Bardewick and Rose, were registered as students in Bologna. Later

on the council of the town several times availed itself of the services
of Wilhelm von Bardewick, who was made a Master in 1302, as
envoy and procurator at the papal court in Rome and Avignon.
There were also many German students in Paris, Orléans, Montpellier and Oxford. From the fourteenth century the sons of
German burghers went to study at Prague, Cologne, Erfurt,
Heidelberg, Vienna and Leipzig. The towns themselves were most
deeply involved in the establishment of universities. This is true
not only of the Italian university towns which, like Bologna, took
over the payment and swearing-in of professors and tried to entice
professors of particular appeal away from other places, but also of
German universities of the late Middle Ages such as Cologne,
Erfurt and Basle. These universities were founded for a great
variety of motives, in the hope of reviving the declining prosperity
of the town, as with Louvain and also Basle; motives of a purely intellectual nature such as Peter von Andlau most purely represented
at the foundation of Basle University; motives of a practical character, the idea of keeping educated clergy, good preachers, men
learned in ecclesiastical and secular law and skilled medical men
within the walls of one town. There was a particular need for
lawyers in fifteenth-century towns, since it had become the custom
that not only were the municipal secretaries and syndics lawyers,
but lawyers also came to enter the council as councillors and
mayors. The North German towns in particular had an astonishingly high number of law students in the fifteenth century. Of the
twenty-three families in control of council seats in Lüneburg,
between 1400 and 1405, more than half their members had studied
law at Prague University; similarly with the good families of Hamburg, Rostock and Lübeck. Lübeck sent a very large number of its
sons to Erfurt and Rostock in the fifteenth century; but Cologne and
Leipzig, and the Italian towns, too, were also visited by the young
men of Lübeck. There certainly was a connection between this
superabundance of academic, above all legal, studies, and the
stagnation of the real artery of the town—enterprising foreign
trade. Hinrich Murmester, who became Mayor of Hamburg in
1467, had studied in Erfurt and Padua. Here he had occupied the
office of Rector, and was made a doctor of laws. We may also

remember the Mayor of Cologne, Johann Hirtz, who was also a doctor; previously he had been active in the university of Cologne as *ordinarius in jure canonico et in decretalibus*.

It had not always been a legal education that decided the issue with the highest municipal officials. The forerunners of the syndics of the fifteenth century were the town clerks, the responsible leaders of the municipal chancelleries who at first only exceptionally had a legal education, as in Lübeck in the middle of the thirteenth century, but were frequently chosen from the ranks of the clergy. Later on, however, the clergy disappeared, and the lawyers included the office of the syndic in that of town clerk.

These town clerks played a glorious part in the literature of their time; they were the born chroniclers of their towns, frequently officially so. Their exact knowledge of official procedures in the town gave their historical works a solid foundation and value; the experiences they gained on their endless diplomatic journeys added to them. If it was in the man's nature, his chronicle turned out narrow and dry; but there are, in contrast, some highly estimable literary achievements, such as the chronicle of the Magdeburg jury clerk Heinrich von Lamspringe, or the Berne chronicles of the town clerk Justinger, who died in 1438. When Piccolomini brought his pupils and followers into the chancelleries of Cologne, Nuremberg and Prague, classicising tendencies set in which were not to the advantage of the chronicles' factual usefulness. Apart from town clerks, the towns themselves encouraged the clergy of the town to write chronicles; thus the work of the Lübeck town clerk Johann Rode (d.1349) was carried on by the Franciscan reading master Detmar, who was commissioned by the councillors of Lübeck. Town histories were also written in verse; we may particularly mention the *Boich van der stede Colne* in which Gottfried Hagen, the town clerk of Cologne, depicted, frequently with passion, in more than 6,000 lines, the struggles between the town and its lords. Burghers of the towns also produced chronicles without being specially commissioned. Augsburg leads in this connection with the names of Burkard Zink (d.1474) and Hektor Mülich (d.1490), of which the former worked his way up to the position of

27   'The Ship of Fools'
From a woodcut by Albrecht Dürer, 1496

a distinguished merchant, while the latter belonged to the big merchant circles by birth.

The remaining literature of the towns gradually freed itself from the pattern of courtly epics and academic-ecclesiastical literature. How strong were the after-effects of the courtly epic can be seen for example in the wall-paintings in a merchant's living-room, discovered in Lübeck, which date from the fourteenth century and whose motifs are taken from the legend of the Grail. The fact that at the same time Johann Wittenborg, a councillor and trader of Lübeck, frequently intersperses the entries in his trading-book with a Latin hexameter the gist of which runs, *Be moderate in all things; moderation is the finest virtue*, clearly indicates how the old knightly ideal of *mâze* (moderation) was bound up with the striving towards mercantile efficiency. On this basis of a reasoned moral pragmatism, burgher literature soon very definitely rejected the old knightly epic and its world. In its place people sought instruction from such a strange book as the Book of Sydrach which, originating in France, was translated into Low German in 1479 in Copenhagen trading circles. It was a catechism of 388 questions and answers on all sorts of things, particularly religious and moral questions. Chess, a favourite game, gave rise to moral reflections; the rules of chess could be given a symbolic interpretation. *The Merchant Company at Business*, a book written in 1475, touches on the practical side of burgher life, and is also interspersed with moral observations. *The Book of the Sea*, which originated in the North Sea area, was a book of instructions for helmsmen of the fifteenth century. But the highest achievement among religious and moral instructional books was *The Ship of Fools* by Sebastian Brant which appeared in 1494, and was one of the best-sellers of its time. In the political reform literature of the fifteenth century a decidedly urban way of thinking is well in evidence in the *Reformatio Sigismundi*, written in 1438. The rise of municipal libraries reflected the growing interest in literature. In this connection Florence led with the foundation of the library in the Dominican monastery of San Marco in 1444; but in 1479 even a town like Hamburg erected a new building for its council library, on whose sculptural decoration a good deal of care and money were lavished.

28   Augsburg in the late fifteenth century

The fact that it was the towns themselves which were the centres
of the great new spiritual movements of Humanism, Renaissance
and Reformation only serves to reflect the leading part played by
towns and *bourgeoisie* in the secularisation of culture at the end of
the period we are dealing with. We may think of Florence in the
late Middle Ages, and of the enormous receptivity of the German
merchants to the Reformation. All this shows how things hang
together; for example, at the turn of the fifteenth and sixteenth
centuries the great commercial activity of Augsburg and Nuremberg within the German towns was matched by a leading position
in the intellectual life of their time. There is a good reason why the
plans of Maximilian I were so closely bound up with Nuremberg
and Augsburg. A man like the Augsburg council syndic Konrad
Peutinger, lawyer, humanist, and much-appreciated adviser of
Maximilian, was better suited than anyone—in his person and with
his house entirely furnished and decorated according to the new ideas
of collecting literary and other kinds of valuable things—to bring
the Emperor into contact with the intellectual-artistic potentiali-

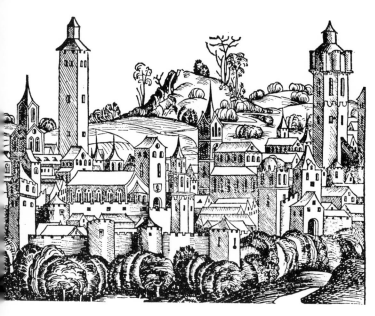

From Schedel, 'Weltkronik', 1493

ties of the South German towns. Names like Willibald Pirckheimer and Albrecht Dürer are sufficient to indicate the association of the Emperor's artistic, genealogical and scientific ambitions with the South German urban culture. But along with Nuremberg and Augsburg we must at least also mention Basle and Strasbourg as foster-homes of the humanist spirit—Basle, on account of its position between the three great regions of culture, was the meeting-place of the humanists in their restless comings and goings, the sphere of influence of Johann Reuchlin and Sebastian Brant, the businessman and lawyer, but above all the human satirist; and finally it was the place which seemed good enough for Erasmus of Rotterdam to choose in 1521 as his final place of residence. Sebastian Brant was syndic in his home town of Strasbourg from 1501. Here in Strasbourg the historical and national characteristics of humanism were underlined in the *Germania*— an argument between Wimpfeling and the Franciscan Thomas Murner; here in a learned dispute Strasbourg's role in the Upper Rhine and in Germany was proclaimed; its splendid, one might even say classical expression in practical politics came with the letters of 1552 from the Strasbourg council to Emperor Charles V.

The fact that Nuremberg, Augsburg, Basle and Strasbourg were at the same time the 'great book-printing towns' is evidence for the way the innumerable elements of urban culture fuse together. When in 1471 the astronomer Regiomontanus was planning to publish on his own account, he chose Nuremberg as his place of residence because it was the centre of European trade. Capital, and the willingness to undertake the new tasks opened up by this new class of merchandise were available here for this 'free' art (in the sense of its not being bound to any guild or union). Even the humanists, such as that excellent man Johann Amerbach in Basle, put themselves at the disposal of the great new task. The great Basle presses also worked for the most important publisher of the time, Antonius Koberger in Nuremberg, who in 1504 gave up his combined business of printing and publishing to devote himself solely to the latter. Between the years of 1510 and 1525 he had thirty-three works printed in presses in Nuremberg, Hagenau, Strasbourg, Basle, Paris and Lyons. The organisation of his publishing business was correspondingly large; his agencies in Lyons and Paris played a very important part in this, as did his sales at the great fairs of Lyon, Frankfurt, Strasbourg and Leipzig; so too did home sales. As yet there existed no class of sufficiently knowledgeable booksellers. The whole of Europe was supplied by this large-scale publishing concern—we may mention Venice and Milan in the south, Antwerp, Lübeck and Gdansk in the north, Vienna, Prague and Ofen in the east, and Lyon and Paris in the west as important places of distribution for Koberger's theological and learned humanist publications. Over 230 works, some of them very expensive and some in many volumes, are in the list of the eldest Antonius Koberger. In North Germany Lübeck took the lead in the printing of books and in their distribution in the Baltic region. As before, books were obtained from South Germany; in 1512 two Lübeck burghers had the intention of printing the breviary of the Lübeck foundation in Nuremberg, or indeed in any other place where good, pure and unimpeachable type could be had. This is another instance of the reputation held by Nuremberg in the north for what concerned the supply of quality goods and products.

The commercial and intellectual interests of the medieval towns-men were inextricably interwoven. Between the time when writing came to be used in business and municipal government, in the thirteenth century, and the large-scale organisation of the tech-nical mass-production of writing through printing and publishing there lies a splendid age of intellectual and commercial effort. Strong though the ties of these people were with the church, this was not allowed to hold up the secularisation of culture in the towns themselves. But since the church itself could not free itself from the after-effects of post-Hellenic astrological influences, it is not surprising that the upper middle classes, and the nobility, were under the spell of strongly held astrological notions. The question of how far the terrible epidemics of plague of the fourteenth and fifteenth centuries were determined by the position of the stars was energetically debated in chronicles, and also in the private letters of merchants and syndics on their travels. Similarly there was a great interest in astrological manuscripts and books. We must stress, however, that the North German chroniclers were not very interested in the notion of the Great Death having been deter-mined by astrological factors; Sebastian Brant also rejected the tendency of his contemporaries to regulate their daily life accord-ing to the 'course of the planets' as being unworthy of a Christian. Melanchthon managed to combine the philosophy of the influence of the planets with a Christian philosophy. Astrological inclinations and commercial speculation were intricately interwoven in the person of Christof Kurz from Nuremberg, who in 1543 and 1544 furnished reports from Antwerp to the Tucher trading company—he believed he was in possession of an astrological system by means of which he could predict the spice prices fourteen days ahead!

The great number of craftsmen and shopkeepers stood in sharp contrast to the merchants and the patricians. Not that the gap could not be bridged—there was no official distinction in the legal sense; but the gap was a social and economic one which, as far as the worker was concerned, involved rights which belonged only to the patrician and the merchant, as for example the right to serve on the council. It was quite possible for a man to move from the working class into the merchant class. Many a distinguished merchant family's name bears witness to the fact that the founder of the family must at one time have been a manual worker. The transition was made at an early age. A bright young man springing from working-class circles was taken up into a merchant's business, had the opportunity of advancing himself in the business, and found his way—probably by means of an arrangement whereby his boss, as a sleeping partner helped him to achieve independence with a small grant of capital—into the merchant class or even into the patriciate. This kind of advancement was frequent in the time of colonisation. It often happened for instance that a young man came to Lübeck from Warendorf in Westphalia, and was there taken into the business of one of the older distinguished 'Warendorp' families and subsequently to continue on his own account.

Taken as a whole there existed between the workers and the merchants a contrast which in these pages has been seen again and again from the latter's point of view. The merchant, following a tradition which went back to earliest times, was an itinerant foreign trader; he was not a local middleman who only supplied what was absolutely necessary in raw materials and goods that could not be manufactured in the town, in order to keep the town's own economy going. It was quite a different story with the worker. His field was not the world, but primarily the market of his own town. The goods the merchant procured from foreign parts aroused the suspicion and ill-will of the manual worker. In his view he could have satisfied local needs just as well with his own goods; but that was his view, not that of the buying public. This is the reason why quality goods which came from outside, and of which the local shopkeeper and worker had no specialised knowledge, were generally retailed by the same wholesale traders who procured the goods. We may remember the 'cutting rights' of the valuable Flemish materials held by the leading men of the wholesale and foreign trade in the German towns which lasted until a circle of local retailers having specialised knowledge, and devoting itself to the retailing of Flemish cloths, was formed, which allowed the wholesale traders progressively to renounce their 'cutting rights'. This happened in Lübeck in the fourteenth century. We may also remember such a large-scale business as that of Antonius Koberger the publisher, with his agents in Paris and Lyons, who at the same time systematically sent out men who had been specially schooled in the job of retailing the published works. Finally there were those Nuremberg merchants in the Hansa who also retailed their richly varied collection of Italian silks, their valuable silver and golden ornaments decorated with jewels, and found a receptive market for them. But one can also understand the troubled complaint of the Lübeck shopkeepers to their council about 1400 that a Nuremberg merchant in Lübeck sold twenty times as much as any other, and as much in one day as a Lübecker did in a year!

If the shopkeeper was the sworn enemy of free trade for foreign merchants in his own town, and would have liked to see their wholesale selling limited, things were different for the workers—or at least more complicated. For it was not only the local market which determined the selling conditions for medieval urban trades. Certainly the provision trades—bakers and butchers—had their circle of customers in the town itself. But even the shoemakers also worked for export, as for instance those of Lübeck worked for the Norwegian market. This was even more true of the metal-working trades of towns like Nuremberg whose products in this field had a good and widespread reputation. The textile trade was least concerned with the home market—particularly in those places whose products had a world-wide reputation, such as the Flemish towns or Florence. The linen and fustian weavers in the small South German towns near Lake Constance, and the linen weavers in Saxon and Lusatian towns also worked for consumers they did not know, who might be hundreds of miles away. However, it was not the worker's job actually to supply the goods to the consumers, but that of commerce. The framework of the relation between worker and merchant was a system of credit which could often bring about the complete dependence of the worker on the merchant, as was the case in Flemish towns and in Florence. It was as no more than a reaction against such grave abuses—in cases where the weavers' enmity towards the merchant upper class in the large

weaving towns was especially strong—that the most bloody conflicts ensued, even though the economic interests of these same
groups of workers were related not to the urban but to the world
market. Relationships were better where the merchant with capital did not make contracts with individual workers but with a
whole union, where it was thus a question of collective contracts.
The first instance known of such a contract was in 1424—between
the Lübeck amber-turners and a group of merchants for the selling
of the greatest part of their production; Venice, Nuremberg,
Frankfurt am Main and Cologne were the projected selling areas.
The manual worker was really best off if he was himself in a position to carry on outside sales. But this was only possible for a few
workers who produced quite valuable wares. Goldsmiths from
Cologne, Augsburg and Nuremberg went in great numbers to the
Frankfurt fair, where they found their best buyers in the international wholesale trade which was there to buy in bulk. But the
trade of goldsmith counted as the most elevated trade in any case;
it was no coincidence that many members of this trade transferred
to the merchant upper class. Nor that the only surviving business
book of a medieval manual worker belonged to a goldsmith. This
was Stefan Maignow, who died in 1500, a man who failed to attain
the degree of importance and artistic skill possessed by his colleagues in Nuremberg, Augsburg and Cologne, but who had
numerous customers among the noble families in the region of
Constance who bought eagerly from him, even if they were not
quite so keen on paying up.

Shopkeepers and those workers who, unlike the weavers, were
economically independent and mainly interested in the local
market were, with their xenophobic tendencies, the real eulogists
of the urban economy. Their aim was to assure all the advantages
of the local market for local people and to organise foreigners'
selling in such a way that local trade should not be at any disad-
vantage on account of it—the foreign merchant, if they had their
way, would only have been permitted to sell wholesale. In this way
he was robbed of a large number of potential customers in the
town; moreover, on account of the prohibition on business with
foreigners, he was eventually dependent on unions and shopkeepers

as his only customers. They were, therefore, exceptionally favoured. Yet the simple fact that trade dominated the economic, social and even political aspects of the more important medieval towns meant that such aims remained unrealised, or were only tolerated and partially achieved later on. Even the economically independent worker was himself in all ways dependent on the merchants, and on the merchant-dominated council. A Lübeck master-baker baked his bread in a bakery belonging to one or other of the old families, sold it in the booths by St Mary's church, which were at the disposal of the council, and lived in a house for which, as a rule, he paid a percentage to a distinguished merchant, or for which, as in Cologne, he only paid rent. Although the individual worker was of no consequence by comparison with the ruling families, the organised association of the workers of any particular trade was.

For this reason alone the development of the guild is one of the most important problems in the history of the German town; it is highly improbable in view of the element of necessary compromise and the variety of individual development that in Germany, or in Europe, it was solved by equal bargaining by the three parties involved—the lord of the town, its council and the workers themselves. In the towns of Flanders and Brabant, where a thoroughgoing sovereign power soon gained influence on working conditions alongside the patrician council, several attempts at a solution were made within a small area. Nevertheless, for Germany, the following characteristics of the development may claim a certain validity. To begin with it was the lord of the town who, aided by his supporters within the town, exercised what was frequently a very effective ruling power over the trades; the best examples of this are the regulations of the older town laws of the lord of Strasbourg. Very soon, as early as the twelfth century, the developing merchant councils exercised similar functions, above all the control of the provision trades and the market. Limitations as to the number of members in a particular trade resulted less from the efforts of the workers themselves than from the official power of the authorities. This was due either to the fact that a fixed number of trading concessions were officially granted to the members of a trade when the town was founded—as happened in

Strehlen, Silesia, in 1292, where thirty-four butchers' stalls, thirty-two bread stalls and thirty cobblers' stalls were set up with the express condition that this number was not to be exceeded—or to the fact that the town council wished to limit the numbers in a particular trade for other reasons such as control, or even punishment. In Lübeck in the fourteenth century the council reduced the number of needle-makers to fourteen and the butchers from 100 to 50 because of their part in disturbances. In the earliest documents which determine the relations between the government and the traders, it was an important fact that the authorities disposed of and supervised everything concerning the trades. Nevertheless as soon as the members of a trade claimed and received the right to belong to a group recognised by the authorities, wide opportunities were opened up for their initiative and effort by means of which they could build up their groups in a way both useful and advantageous to the members. The occasional limits on the number of members of a trade by the authorities at the same time gave very valuable economic privileges to the lucky ones who were left in; only those authorised could practise a trade. This also meant compulsory membership of a guild—and without membership no-one could ply his trade. Only the authorities could grant this right; they also decided whether and how far the guild might exercise its own jurisdiction over offences against the constitution of the guild or its regulations.

The guild could only retain its charter if it gave the authorities no excuse to intervene. If the interests of the buying townspeople were damaged through the exploitation of the guild's preferential position the guild might be dissolved, as the bakers and butchers of Erfurt found in 1264. In such cases the council at the very least would appoint free masters. On account of this ever-present threat, but also certainly on account of a feeling of duty towards the honour of the trade, the older guild ordinances in particular lay great stress on their obligation to protect the customer. Again and again, whether in Basle or Berlin, in Regensburg or Soest, concern for the quality of the goods is particularly stressed as being the main purpose of the guilds, in guild documents of the thirteenth century. They were also concerned that a good product should be

sold at a fair price. In order to achieve both these aims, the process
of production was supervised from the buying of the raw materials
to the selling of the goods. A careful training of the future master
as a journeyman and assistant, and the preparation of the master-
piece as proof of sufficient ability also worked in the same direction.
Of course the training and its termination could be wilfully interfered with (as sometimes occurred later on) in order to make
acceptance more difficult and in order to keep out new competitors.
This leads us to consider those measures taken by the guilds in the
interests of their members. Here, in guild circles, there actually
existed that spirit which it would be a mistake to look for in the
whole economic life of the town—the striving after a burgher
livelihood. 'Trades were introduced so that everyone could earn
his daily bread from them' runs the so-called *Reformatio Sigismundi*
of 1438. The aim was not a general levelling of incomes, but, where
possible, to do so within a particular trade. On this account every
member was supposed as far as possible to have the same working
conditions in buying raw materials, working hours, number of
assistants and shops. And because of this any attempt to advertise,
or to tempt customers away from another man, was strictly forbidden in the guilds.

However, not all the provisions of the guild regulations were
entirely effective. In spite of all the regulations there were rich
workers and poor workers. Where the guild and its inclinations
most prevailed it was not to the advantage of the town. The case
of Freiburg im Breisgau is effective warning against overestimating
the guild economy—for this, and not urban economy, is what it
should be called, since the urban economy in reality remained
far more influenced by commerce and economic aims opposed to
guild interests. Here, where once distinguished merchants had
laboured to establish the town, the old foreign trade connections
of the town were cut in pieces after the victory of the guilds around
1470 ('with great rapidity and with results that were carried too
far') and the town strove after economic self-sufficiency. Along
with trade the formation of capital was depressed. It all came down
to the regulation of competition amongst the workers by themselves; each worker became an official suspiciously observing the

29 Cologne in the late fifteenth century

From a woodcut by Anton Woensam, 1523

other. Whoever lived in the town had to be organised in some way. It was only carrying the policy to its logical conclusion when the town itself was 'closed' in the same way that the guilds had been 'closed'—that is by having their membership restricted—the entry of foreigners into the town was made more difficult by increasing the guild and civic taxes. The result was that the old town of Freiburg which in 1385 had between 9,000 and 9,500 inhabitants decreased in size until in 1500 it had about 5,700; the number of houses diminished by a third, houses were turned into gardens and in the years between 1494 and 1520 between one-seventh and one-eighth of the entire housing came under the hammer! Even in some of the most important trading towns, such as Basle or Cologne the guilds' economic aims gained ground towards the end of the Middle Ages. In 1521 a series of reforms took place in Basle, likewise at the expense of commerce which made all foreign competition with local products impossible. In Cologne too, though to a lesser degree, concessions were made to the guilds' economic programme—in every case visibly harming the economic importance of the towns. But Nuremberg—the healthiest of late medieval towns—knew how to suppress the influence of the guilds on its economy. It was not an 'urban economy' but a free-trade economy that Nuremberg had to thank for its dominant position. And nobody fared better than the trades themselves in the process. The merchant-appointed council pressed for the highest quality in craft products, but at the same time, by virtue of its commercial efforts, it guaranteed for them more of a world market than a local one.

In economic matters, the supposed harmony of the medieval town was broken by sharp differences between the commercial and the working classes. Obviously this contrast was reflected in the political field; the guildsmen could only achieve practical realisation of their economic ideal if they shared in membership of the council, or occupied all of it themselves. The conflicts between guilds and patriciate often began in political terms—the guilds formed the core of the resistance to the actual or alleged financial mismanagement of the council. The story of the Flemish towns has shown with what bitterness these conflicts were fought out; here, too, the inseparability of political, economic and social aims within the opposing classes is clear. The conflicts also took a particularly acute form in German towns which had a large number of weavers—Cologne and Brunswick for example. Almost everywhere in the south-western towns in the thirteenth and fourteenth centuries the guilds gained some degree of a share in the government of the town. Sometimes they were directly represented by councillors on a council which had previously been the exclusive preserve of the leading families; at other times there were two councils in existence at the same time, the old and the new; in which case the constitution provided that the new council should be consulted on certain questions concerning the town. It also happened that the previous council was completely abolished so that the guilds formed the group from which the new council was to be elected. This occurred in Cologne in 1396, when twenty-two political guilds or *Gaffeln* were formed for election to the council. In each of these one of the commercial guilds was the main guild with which the others were associated. The first group was known as the weavers guild, along with related trades; it had the largest number of councillors to elect—four. The remaining twenty-one groups elected thirty-two between them. A further forty-four representatives of the groups were to be called in on the more important matters. All the inhabitants of the town who were not members of a guild—which included also the merchants and leading families—had to associate themselves with one of the groups. Radical as this change of constitution appears, it turned out in practice to be less so. Actually it was still the merchants and not the workers who ruled in Cologne after 1396—although they were prepared to make all kinds of concessions to the lower classes.

This was true of most of the larger trading towns in the fifteenth century. In a town like Lübeck, where the constitutional demands of the workers and those merchants who did not belong to the select families were not met, and where it became clear, at the beginning of the fifteenth century, that the workers simply could not do without the leading families' centuries-long experience in foreign politics, the leading class went an extraordinarily long way towards meeting the economic wishes of the workers and shopkeepers. In German towns the weaver proleteriat did not have anything like the importance it did in Flanders, and independent master-craftsmen, often of sound economic standing, stood alongside the patriciate; even so a *rapprochement* was all the more possible because towards the end of the fifteenth century the upper section of guild-masters, which also had a share in the municipal offices, was terrified by the growing ill-will amongst the depressed population. Journeymen who could not manage to become masters, day-labourers and people who had to earn their bread without the protection of a guild played a dangerous role in this. Their fury was directed both against the patriciate and the guild-masters who ruled alongside them. Resentment over increasing burdens imposed on the small man by the monied classes through indirect taxation already mingled with the simple hate borne by the have-nots towards the haves. The council of Erfurt fled before this hate in 1509; in 1513 seven Cologne councillors ended up on the scaffold. Strasbourg, after dramatic struggles and endless compromises between the upper class and the guilds, had arrived in 1482 at a permanent constitutional reform of finely calculated equilibrium, and with its cautious financial politics and the goodwill of all groups participating in its apparently democratic, but in fact oligarchic constitution, appeared to the leading spirits of around 1500 like an oasis in the desert. In the famous words of Erasmus, he believed he could see here a monarchy without a tyrant, an aristocracy without factions, a democracy without uproar, wealth without luxury and happiness without presumption.

Something of the romantic aura with which ideas about medieval guilds are surrounded seems to shine forth in these words. It would in fact be wrong when discussing the guild to speak only about struggles for economic and political importance. In those towns where the ruling classes lost something of their acquisitive urge and replaced it with the ideal of living from unearned income, and where perseverance was at a premium, an internal political mood existed which guaranteed the worker living conditions such that he was relieved of the trouble of struggling for existence and, provided he was personally able, could achieve some extraordinarily good things. This is the explanation of the urban

30   The town gate

From an illuminated history of Charlemagne, 1460
Bibliothèque Royale, Brussels, MS. 9066

31   A town scene in the fifteenth century
Bibliothèque Nationale, Paris, MS. français 288, f. 198

art which was so eminent in the medieval town and which we admire today, and the products of which we find continually in the cultural circle of the urban patriciate. We may remind ourselves once again of that great achievement of German industry, the invention of printing with movable letters. As a free art it did not allow itself to be coerced by the guilds, but entered into those connections we have already indicated—on the one hand, with the foreign-trading entrepreneurs of publishing, and on the other, with the artistic and scholarly forces of the time. One only has to remember how the German woodcut flourished at the turn of the century! Certainly the creative artist felt only too strongly the narrowness of the world dominated by the guilds in which he found himself. We may mention the difficulties experienced by Peter Vischer with the rapid advances in the specialisation of work and the monopolies of individual specialised trades, for which the related metal trades were responsible; we may also mention what Albrecht Dürer wrote to his friend Pirkheimer from Venice: 'How cold I shall be after the sun; here I am a lord, and at home a sponger'. The feeling certainly also imbued with the fear of those strict limits within which the life of an artist was lived at home.

The guild was more than just an economic federation for its members; it embraced their whole external life. The guild had its saint, whose memory was celebrated by all the members together, and for whom an altar was established and maintained in the church. Christian charity was shown towards members fallen on hard times. The bier of a departed member was covered with cloths and palls belonging to the guild, and carried by other members to the grave. Evidently the social life with its strong tendencies towards excess in eating and drinking played a special role. Gay times were also had in the guildhalls of the manual workers. The workers' military duty also overflowed into the political—parts of the municipal fortifications were given to individual guilds to defend.

Although the workers' unions were local organisations, which tried to regulate and supervise the whole life of their members, nevertheless there was no lack of inter-urban federations within the same trade. The single coopers' roll for Lübeck, Hamburg,

Wismar and Greifswald of 1321 stems from the Hanseatic merchants' interests in the activity of these coopers in Scania during the
herring catches. Later on individual guilds of various towns—for
instance Frankfurt, Mainz, Worms, Speyer, Heidelberg and
Koblenz—made agreements amongst themselves, designed to
establish consistent regulation of the working conditions of journeymen and workers. At the beginning of the sixteenth century it was
agreed between the smiths of Lübeck and Riga that journeymen
who had not done well in one town should not be engaged in the
other. One trade even regulated the affairs of *all* its members *in
dütschen Landen*. This was the stonemasons' guild, whose itinerant
members, from the masters down to the journeymen and helpers,
were the creators of the great public buildings. They agreed on this
ordinance for the whole of Germany, from Strasbourg and Berne,
from Basle and Esslingen to Passau and Vienna, in Regensburg in
1459.

32   The earliest illustration of a printing press
From a woodcut in a French 'Danse Macabre', 1499

8

POWER AND
INSTITUTIONS

❋

Planning and leadership on the part of the ruling classes in the town was the prerequisite of almost everything we have dealt with up to now. Their legal basis was the town's autonomy, and their organ the council. When the competence of the council, which stemmed from the right first granted to it—that of settling disputes in the market—was territorially extended over the whole area of the town and, functionally, to the whole or to the majority of those matters once exercised by the lord of the town or his agents, the council became a completely new governmental organisation which seems modern even today. In this system of government the role of central committee fell to the council, while special committees developed to deal with special problems of government. The united policy of these individual committees was however guaranteed by the fact that their chairmen took part in the meetings of the council as councillors. Here again we can see the importance of the town in influencing the political organisation of the larger states which were formed subsequently, so that it has made no difference to Germany whether and how far the states directly imitated the achievements of the towns. In Frankfurt am Main in 1450 there were eighteen such council committees, mostly consisting of six or three members which reflected the distribution of political power in the council itself—jurymen, patricians and guilds. In towns ruled purely by the leading families, patrician councillors were at the head of the individual offices. The council, as a whole, and the special committees all had their paid officials. The highest was the town clerk, a highly respected official who was head of the municipal chancery, keeper of the court books and records, and finally ambassador of the town. He had a whole series of minor officials under him, as officials of the central executive run by the mayors, although very soon the committees required their own clerks, chanceries and special officials, from the market bailiff to the executioner. The council members themselves were unpaid—which did not mean that they could not avail themselves of all the allowances and privileges provided by the town—for example free food for the ruling mayor and his guests, and extra allowances of all kinds, including travel allowances. These could give rise to envy and corruption.

Literacy and money, achievements of the townsmen themselves, were indispensable for the new kind of government. They made it possible, above all, to build up taxation and a system of public credit which facilitated that extraordinary advance of the town in financial matters which, at least in Germany, did not relax throughout the whole of the Middle Ages, though the governments of the medieval towns never got as far as the formal estimate or budget.

With the transference of regular direct taxation from the lord of the town to the town itself municipal autonomy in financial matters began. The lord of the town (in imperial towns the emperor) received an agreed lump sum; once this was paid the town could do as it liked as far as taxation was concerned. Direct taxation based on wealth or income was developed; limits were set to this by the conditions prevailing in other towns: over-taxation could result in the emigration of those affected. Property was the main object of direct taxation. But the rates were not particularly high—they were mostly less than one per cent; and when in Brunswick in 1388 a rate of 2·1 per cent was demanded this represented an unusually high rate determined by special circumstances. It was a serious matter that additional taxes demanded as 'advances' (as for example in Augsburg in 1475) tended to become progressively harsher on those lower down the social scale. A similar effect obtained for example in Nuremberg in 1431 with the Hussite taxes or with the Basle property taxes. Of the many supplementary taxes that existed we can only mention one here, a very remarkable arrangement introduced by the council of Metz in the fourteenth century under the pressure of wartime emergencies—an arrangement which to start with was temporary, but which, like so many, was never rescinded afterwards. This was the taxation of all monies transferred by document: at a rate of less than one per cent to start with, but at two and a half per cent after 1363. Private documents of transference were then only fully valid as proof of payment when the sealed receipt of the tax committee was affixed. In addition, all these revenues were entered in a public register after 1379. Indirect taxes also played a major role in municipal accounting. The percentage of revenues they represented increased from the fourteenth to the fifteenth centuries, and frequently exceeded the revenue from direct taxation by a considerable margin. In the fourteenth century Cologne even gave up direct taxation altogether and revenues from indirect taxation amounted to 95.7 per cent of the regular income. No wonder the small people of the town who were particularly affected by indirect taxation felt themselves oppressed. Moreover, taxation of the largest incomes in the town was regulated by contracts very favourable to the people being taxed. False declarations were not exactly infrequent—people did not like paying taxes. In 1418 a tax collector of Constance remarked of a taxpayer, 'So much should he pay—which he seldom does. He will look pretty sour when I catch up with him.'

But it frequently happened that the regular revenues of the town were insufficient, and debts were incurred. To start with the town was able to make revenues out of urban property. Annuity contracts with the city treasurer became increasingly popular, too. When in 1405 there was trouble over the financial management of the Lübeck council, it turned out that between 1394 and 1405 the council had increased the revenue debt by 71,080 Lübeck marks—the buying power of which would today represent about one million pounds. Between 1368 and 1396 Lübeck creditors had bought urban investments in Lüneburg for about 50,000 Lübeck marks, and the town of Lübeck itself had about 25,000 Lübeck marks outstanding from Lüneburg. These figures indicate very clearly how much capital there was in Lübeck at the time seeking investment which was eagerly accepted not only by Lübeck itself, but also in the neighbouring town. Even Swedish capitalists, among them the Vadstena monastery, were glad to invest their money in Lüneburg bonds through their confidential agents in Lübeck.

A glance at the expenditure side of medieval municipal accounts illustrates further tasks of the municipal government. Expenditure on defence was very high. In Cologne in 1379 about eighty-two per cent of the total expenditure went on the defence of the town. The sum was in the region of 81,000 Cologne marks—again a sum which today would represent millions sterling. A good deal of this amount was swallowed up by fortifications; a fair amount went to pay the knights and squires, and in gratuities to the so-called 'noble' burghers, distinguished gentlemen who were supposed to have an interest in the special protection of the itinerant merchants of Cologne. But it was not as though the towns only defended themselves with the help of knightly and other mercenaries. The burgher was also compelled to play his part, and the upper class to provide warhorses and full armour. A town like Nuremberg in the fifteenth century had a very well organised and equipped army at its disposal with all kinds of weapons. The artillery, a force which cannot be organised without a rich and well-ordered government, was thus the towns' main advantage over their princely opponents in the fourteenth and fifteenth centuries. Strasbourg was renowned for its riflemen, and the Hanseatic towns had their own very good reason for preventing the export of guns from the town to the countryside. In the 1340's the folk-singer warned those princes who had banded together in a discreditable enterprise against the town of Magdeburg in a song about the Magdeburg war establishment:

> Give ear to me, you princes high,
> For I advise you faithfully
> To keep the town as your ally—
> They have such good artillery;
> With guns that shoot so rapidly.

The attack on Magdeburg was carried out and resulted in a heavy defeat for the attacking princes.

A further weapon which only the towns possessed was the warship. All the naval exploits performed on the German side up to and during the sixteenth century—and there are plenty of them—were performed by fleets which were fitted out by the coastal towns, manned by them and captained by their councillors. Naval skill and readiness to engage in naval battle were one of the conditions of Hanseatic greatness. The Hansa achieved much politically. Even when, as in the first (and until the tragic year of 1914 the only) naval war between Germany and England, the military results of the privateers' wars were not always in favour of the Hansa, and economic warfare then turned out to be no longer really practicable. The main reason for the Hansa's success lies not only in the complete subordination of military affairs to political leadership, but also in their ability to rejoin the threads of negotiation at any time, even during the fighting, and to complete the negotiations successfully by means of inherently self-assured and consistent diplomatic skill. We can thus understand why at the negotiations of Utrecht in 1473, which brought the Hanseatic-English naval war to an end, the chief English negotiator conceded full victory to Hanseatic diplomacy with the words: 'I would rather negotiate with all the princes in the world than with envoys of the Hanseatic council.' We can understand too why the Mayor of Lübeck, Hinrich Castorp, in spite of all military preparations, gave the maxim for Hanseatic politics as: 'Let us negotiate! For it is easy to tie the pennant to the pole, but hard to take it down again with honour.' They could afford to negotiate for the simple reason that they knew they were masters in the diplomatic game.

Closely connected with the defence measures of the towns in the late Middle Ages were their efforts to form a municipal territory which as far as possible should enclose a series of strongholds. The more the princes endeavoured to extend their rights over an enclosed area, and the more the princes' integrated territorial state became reality, the more understandable became the towns' efforts to keep as large as possible an area around the town out of the clutches of neighbouring princes. The towns had previously attempted to exert an influence on the surrounding countryside. Since the thirteenth century, merchants and ecclesiastical founda-

33   Magdeburg in the late fifteenth century

From Schedel, 'Weltkronik', 1493

tions led by middle-class agents had been acquiring property, revenues and rights of jurisdiction in the countryside, sometimes scattered over a wide area and sometimes adjacent. Thus in the period before 1350, in pursuit of its policy of assuring the corn supply, Lübeck acquired about four-fifths of the total hides of the island of Poel near Wismar, an island famous for its excellent corn lands; the produce of the manors together with the corn to be disposed of in private trade went to Lübeck. By this time Lübeck had acquired all kinds of rights in at least 240 villages as far afield as Wolgast, Rügen and Fehmarn in the east and north-east. From then on began the friction with the minor agents of the lords of the various regions where these acquisitions had been made; the separate territorial states, becoming self-conscious, were no longer prepared to tolerate the penetration of foreign townsmen exercising sovereign rights. Now came the time when the town moved towards the building up of a territory which should as far as possible exclude all alien sovereign rights, in order to defend itself against the danger that was clearly threatening. The example of Nuremberg indicates how this desire for an independent territory could develop into a centuries-long struggle with princely opponents, in this case the Franconian Hohenzollerns. At the turn of the fourteenth and fifteenth centuries Rothenburg, under its energetic mayor, Heinrich Toppler, carried out a far-reaching territorial policy of exceptional proportions, which involved in particular the acquisition of fortified houses; but with the decline of the community could not be maintained against the advancing power of the princes. In the west, Metz created a well-ordered urban territory for itself. The urban territorial formations of the Hansa have been maintained in their rudiments on the map of Germany to the present day. The territorial policy of Erfurt, an evident defence measure against princely territorialism, had managed by the end of the fifteenth century to create a region which included, apart from Erfurt, the small town of Sömmerda and eighty-three villages. The territory belonging to the town had an area of about 610 square kilometres and, including the town itself, between 42,000 and 50,000 inhabitants. The part of Germany where the formation of 'city-states' occurred most successfully was Switzerland; here the formation of princes' states which was successful in the rest of Germany, was nipped in the bud. Zürich, Berne and Lucerne in particular soon became city-states politically dominating the surrounding countryside. In 1501, when Basle joined the Swiss Confederation it brought with it considerable territory which had been founded in 1400 by the acquisition of domains belonging to the Bishop of Basle, who had got into debt. Obviously, Italy remains the classical land of European city-states; it was the relationship between city and state in France, England, Spain and Scandinavia which prevented the emergence of city-states in those countries.

In a time of declining imperial power the territorial policy of the town outside its walls was inextricably bound up with its military activities, and the building activities within the town were strongly affected by the military considerations. This was particularly true of the city walls themselves. These are what give the medieval town its highly characteristic aspect—within the walls the loosely huddled mass of houses, and outside the walls, on account of their military purpose, generally nothing at all; at the most there were buildings which could be sacrificed in the event of an enemy attack, in order not to provide him with a strong-point. An example of a town in which the walls represented a sharp break between the two opposites—in front of them empty ground and behind the densely populated area of the town—can still be seen in Wisby, on Gotland, with its oriental, fairy-tale circle of fortifications. In France we can mention the solid ring wall built in 1240–46 around Aigues-Mortes in the salt lakes west of the Rhone estuary, with its gate-towers, built as part of the crusading plans of Louis IX. It enclosed the most important Mediterranean trading port of France in the thirteenth century. The French monarchy certainly raised Aigues-Mortes consciously for its own political purposes. In Germany we can mention the great achievement of the fortifications of Rothenburg which with the position of the town on a plateau was incomparably important. But above all we must mention the huge wall constructed by the townsmen of Cologne in the twelfth and thirteenth centuries; even if a hasty extension of the town in the nineteenth century has left behind only a few gate-towers, robbed of their organic context. Metz in the west, Nuremberg in the south

34 Attack on a fortified town   *From an engraving by Albrecht Dürer, 1527*

and Reval in the east still provide splendid examples of medieval urban fortifications. From the time when the towns' enemies gradually learned to make use of artillery themselves, the military significance of the town gates retained only a symbolic character. Nevertheless in the fifteenth and sixteenth centuries the towns vied with each other in dignified receptions for foreign visitors as soon as they set foot in the town by means of an artistic elaboration of the gates. Even small and very small towns were not to be left behind in this direction; buildings in brick produced an abundance of valuable artistic solutions. The Stargarder gate in Neubrandenburg and the Lübeck castle gate are only two examples of this.

The same sense of dignity and show was to be found in the central building of the municipal government—the town hall. This too was something that was formed through centuries, and expanded according to its functions. At first, until far into the thirteenth century, the cloth house, that is, the place where cloth was sold, was the most important public building in the town. In some towns, like Lübeck and Torun, the council left the insignificant house or room, which had been good enough for private deliberations, and went over to the cloth house in the thirteenth century; in Lübeck when, before 1250, two warehouses were built parallel to each other, the council moved into the first storey of the house built on the Breitenstrasse. From the end of the thirteenth century, that is, from the time when writing began to play a part in jurisdiction and government, the space required for the council and government grew visibly—then the whole of the foremost of the two houses became the town hall. In the fourteenth century the town hall grew along the Breitenstrasse northwards and southwards. In the fifteenth century the southwards extension was finished off by that building which contains the lavish 'war chamber'. To the north there was no halt in expansion until 1614 when the chancery building was put up. These extensions to the town hall drove the small trade out of the market and replaced market buildings with government buildings. One of the grandest town halls, that of the old town of Torun built at the end of the fourteenth century, incorporated the various older buildings already in existence in the market place, which had served as market, court and government buildings, by its original system of huge enclosing walls. In its solid, turreted, castle-like compactness this town hall reminds one more of the Palazzo Vecchio, the town hall of Florence built about 1300, than of other German town halls, most of which are not single self-sufficient buildings, but complexes made up of different origin and purpose. The when and how of the origin of the most salient parts of these complexes determine the effect of the whole and thus account for that abundance of solutions and outward forms displayed by the German town hall. In Brunswick the two wings of the town hall in the old town, built at the beginning and at the end of the fourteenth century, were joined into a richly decorative unit by a two-storied covered way. In other town halls, such as those of Regensburg, Nuremberg and Wrocław, one can see clearly how parts of the building constructed at widely different times have grown together. Where it was not possible to extend the town hall, special buildings were constructed for the chancery, and even for the assembly hall.

Town walls, town halls, the trade halls of Flanders, armouries, granaries, and bridges, most architecturally outstanding in Nuremberg, clearly indicate the role played by the municipal control of building in the Middle Ages. From the thirteenth century onwards it was a municipal building committee which constructed the whole of Bruges in the subsequent centuries. It fixed the rows of buildings with a deliberate, even exaggerated stress on differences in balustrades; it looked after the paving of the roads and the water supply of the town; it encouraged the replacement of thatched roofs in favour of tiled roofs through a kind of bonus system; and in short it intervened in everything. The planning and layout of the whole town was also, at least in the great new foundations of the twelfth century, the result of burgher initiative and building. Practical and rational as these town plans seem to us, aesthetic considerations were not forgotten either right from the start. For it is not by pure chance that we get again and again in the Middle Ages such wonderful street-endings—here a church façade or there a group of market and town hall buildings; all this would not have been possible if the streets had not been planned from the beginning in such a way that our gaze falls continually on the buildings stretched out in front of us, and never gets lost in the bleak emptiness of a dead-straight open-ended street. A more exact study of the medieval town as an organic unity throws up some surprising facts in this connection. The most important people in charge of building were the master-builders who carried out the construction as municipal officials. In a town like Nuremberg one can trace everywhere the hand of the master-builder Hans Behaim the Elder, who died in 1538 having served the town for forty-eight years; it is thanks to him that at the turn of the fifteenth and sixteenth centuries the Gothic style could flourish strongly again in the secular architecture of Nuremberg.

Merchant artistic creation in the towns has been strikingly triumphant, particularly with regard to church building. This is above all true of the urban parish churches. The St Mary's churches in Lübeck and Gdansk in the north and the cathedrals of Freiburg and Ulm in the south are outstanding examples of this urban ecclesiastical building activity. The burghers supplied the building materials, and the master-builders under contract from the council carried it out. The burghers were also directly involved in the strongholds of ecclesiastical building, the proud cathedrals of the episcopal towns. As early as the thirteenth century the council of Siena was responsible for the building of the cathedral. In Strasbourg too the council took over responsibility for building the cathedral; in 1395 there even occurred, through the mediation of the emperor, an agreement by which the council became the sole building contractor for the cathedral, to the exclusion of the bishop. These large-scale ecclesiastical building projects under municipal administration provided the opportunity for that itinerant band of master-builders and their assistants, the simple masons, to demonstrate their skills; the building site of Strasbourg was their high-school. About 1400 Ulrich von Ensingen left his mark on the layout of the Ulm cathedral, in the towers of the *Liebfrauenkirche* in Esslingen and on the cathedral of Strasbourg. Apart from this Ensingen had also been in Milan for a short time, where the German and Italian building experts were frequently at variance over the building of the cathedral. Members of the Parler family, the famous family of master-builders who had a decisive influence

on the appearance of Prague, also played a part here. There is a
connection between the strong, progressive spirit which dominated Lübeck about 1300 and the mighty soaring stone masses of
the towers of St Mary's. It was works of this kind which released
in Goethe that 'heavenly-earthly joy of embracing the gigantic
spirit of our older brothers in their works'.

But the building of churches was not the only way in which the
municipal authorities encroached upon the ecclesiastical province;
the position of church and clergy within the town continually led
to friction, and created administrative problems. The area of immunity of the cathedral minster within the town, frequently
surrounded by a wall of its own, clearly expressed the legal anti-
nomy between municipal and ecclesiastical life; in Nuremberg the
'area of immunity' and the market, two areas of the town encircled
by their own walls, remained isolated until the nineteenth century.
Ill-feeling arose when the lay inhabitants of the area of immunity
wanted to share the advantages of urban life without shouldering
its burdens. For this reason the municipal authorities about 1300
laid down the principal that 'those who work with the town must
also bear its burdens'—which meant paying the taxes. The towns
sharply resisted any extension of the tax-free properties of churches
and monasteries within the town. Further acquisition of properties
and revenues by *mortmain* were either entirely forbidden, as in
Lübeck and Erfurt, or it was stipulated that the newly acquired
property should be sold to laymen after a year and a day. The
council gained increasing influence in the appointment of parsons
to the parish churches. Frequently, though not everywhere, the
council had control of the living; it also developed a system of
trusteeship over all the clerical benefices in the town—as in Brunswick and Esslingen—and thus got possession of all the extremely
numerous curacies of the individual foundations. Thus the curate
was far more dependent on the town council than on his ecclesiastical superiors; the greater part of the secular clergy consisted of
curates in the innumerable religious institutions. In the light of all
this, it is more understandable that the councils which appointed
their lay agents to churches, monasteries and hospitals, supervised
through these agents their whole financial administration and

35 Brussels: the Town Hall, built 1401–55

36 The Shipping House, built in 1535

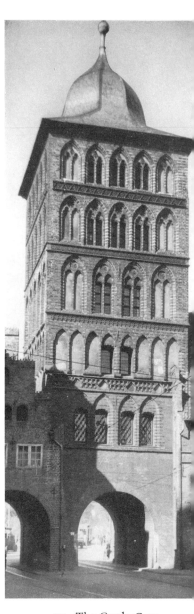

37 The Castle Gate

LÜBECK

directed it according to their own interests, should in the late Middle Ages even interfere in ecclesiastical matters. It was under their initiative that the late medieval reform of monasteries took place, as in Basle in the first half of the fifteenth century, with regard to the Dominicans and Franciscans. It was the same in numerous other towns; Nuremberg and Erfurt were particularly concerned about monastic reform at the historic moment of Luther's journey to Rome. Finally, the council made decrees about Sunday observance and processions, settled quarrels between the parish clergy and the monasteries about the right of free burial, as it did in Basle, and interfered with church discipline—all of which goes to show how far-reaching was the council's control over the spiritual life. The establishment of municipal schools and universities lay in the same hands, as did social welfare, in which the town was more involved than the church. But here, too, there is a great variety in individual cases; there were towns, such as Mainz, which were unable to carry through their demands against the clergy. But on the whole the town had a profound influence over ecclesiastical matters on the eve of the Reformation.

The administrative problems of the medieval town in military and ecclesiastical matters are a clear indication of its sphere of competence, for imperial town and 'country town' alike. There is an immense abundance of information testifying to the astonishing, intensive internal administrative activity of the council. We have already touched on the main features of its trade and commercial policies, and on its legislation on luxury and the burghers' policies of provision for times of need. This policy of provision led early on to large-scale measures; for instance in 1289 (for a sum which today would equal many thousands of pounds) Lübeck acquired the right to dam the Wakenitz and the Ratzeburg lake, thus allowing it to carry out its large-scale plans for watermills. The Wakenitz is actually today still a long, tube-like dam of thirteenth-century origin. Certainly the trade policy which made Lübeck into a corn and flour shipping centre played a part in this. Equally impressive were the Nuremberg granaries which served as storehouses for corn in times of siege. For further functions of the municipal administration, there is the case of the municipal 'moral police' in particular. In the fifteenth century the council of Nuremberg issued a decree against excessively short clothing—and we may note that it was then a question of male dress, whose extravagances in any case provoked other prohibitions—while the fact that this council had to decree prohibitions because 'many unusual, shameful and improper new dances are daily introduced and practised', would lead rather to comparisons with our own post-war years than to the appreciation of medieval administrative activity. There is no doubt that such directives on the part of the police reflected a strong inclination to interfere with anything and everything which had to do with the burghers; it becomes most clear in this connection how far the council of a medieval town represented 'the authorities'. Apart from the provision policies we have already mentioned more than once, we have a better criterion for the large-scale achievements of medieval government in the administration of justice. The laws of one town were taken over by many others. Whole families of urban law were formed in this way. Lübeck and Magdeburg were two supreme courts, in the sense that many towns had adopted their laws. But the greatest permanent achievement of the German town in the field of law was the development of municipal property and revenue books. In Cologne the proud series of *Schreinskarten*, which continued in the property books, began in 1135; the property book of Lübeck was opened in 1224. The oldest has been lost; but it is still possible today to trace back the changes of ownership and revenues of every single piece of ground in the old town of Lübeck to the last two decades of the thirteenth century.

The municipal administration of coinage, an excellent indication of public functions, gave rise to agreements which went far beyond the individual town—the so-called currency agreements. They were defensive measures designed to get rid of the effects of particularistic disunity and thoughtlessness at least in the field of currency; they took the form of binding towns with the right of minting currency to maintain standards of coinage and regulate the kind of coins that might be minted. The towns were the driving force behind these agreements—particularly the Wendic currency federation which, after a number of previous weaker agreements, united

38 Lübeck: one of the city's gateways
From a woodcut of 1560

Lübeck, Hamburg and Wismar in 1379, and was very quickly
extended to a large number of North German towns. This was
true also of the South German currency federations, such as the
Rappenbund, founded in 1403, in which Basle played the leading
role. The towns of Colmar, Breisach and Freiburg joined in, and the
Hapsburg lordships in the neighbourhood were also drawn into it.
The control of currency and the exchange of business was a further
characteristic feature of municipal government and set it many
difficult problems, among which the supply of suitable metal for
the coinage was not the least considerable.

39   Minting coins
From Raphael Holinshed, 'Chronicles', 1577

9

CONCLUSION

❈

The medieval town should not be thought of as a small, self-contained unit, but only within the framework of the organic inter-relationship of towns. Long-distance trade provided the basis on which urban life on the grand scale was founded and prospered. Each town was dependent on another for its functioning; we may remember the relationship of Bruges to Lübeck, or of Lübeck to Riga. It was for this reason that in the literary concept of the urban economy, trade was far more heavily stressed than is usual; if through concentration on a local 'guild economy', a 'closed urban economy' developed, then the town had already lost its main source of strength. All the romantic notions of guild honour and master-singing cannot alter this fact. The history of the urban economy in Germany is by no means to be regarded as something less than the subsequent 'territorial economy' or 'political economy'—on the contrary, the age of prosperous towns rather presupposed factors of a 'world economic' nature. For the fact that Asiatic wares were distributed in Europe by commerce with such regularity and in such large amounts is one aspect of a world economy, as also is the fact that enormous quantities of brass, bronze and copper goods from Nuremberg, Aix and Cologne found their way via Portugal to the negro kingdom of Benin in the fifteenth century.

Only now did the dangers that were threatening in the development of the German state-system become quite clear. It was quite a peculiar circumstance that, as the power of the monarchy declined, the German towns were not able to perpetuate their initial freedom from any territorially defined national structure; it could not have been permanent. In Italy the towns dominated the countryside; city-states of great size bordered on each other. In France and England the monarchy integrated the towns, and subjected them to the developing national state. But in Germany the monarchy under Charles IV abdicated its position as the representative of the idea of the national and recognised the developing state formation of feudalism. Obviously in Germany, too, it had to come to the formation of states; obviously the towns either had to fit into them, as they did in England and France, or they had to dominate the development of these states—the Italian solution. In either case there remained a possibility of shaping the urban economy favourably—we may remember Louis XI of France and the French town, and the Tudors and the English town; we may remember the city-states of Venice, Milan and Florence. The cause of the decline of the German town is not to be found in the fact that it was integrated into a state, but in the fact that it was subjected to a state-system which was both inadequate, and with which it was incompatible. The German system of separatist states, which now became the only system in Germany, was inadequate, if only on account of the smallness and the disunity of these entirely unorganised products of the purely dynastic struggle for power. Not without reason had the struggle for a large, unified area of trade led the towns in earlier centuries to side with the king. If they were subjected to individual territories, as the Hanseatic towns of Brandenburg, were torn 'with an iron hand', out of the Hansa, and thus from their old far-reaching connections, then the foundations of their old greatness were destroyed. From the end of the fourteenth and throughout the following centuries the struggle dragged on between the separatist principalities and the towns, which, to start with, frequently resulted in heavy defeats for the aggressors as in 1389 with the coalition of the Archbishop of Cologne and the Count of the Mark against Dortmund, or the attacks on Lüneburg of 1370 and 1396. It was the Hohenzollerns who won the first significant successes in the struggle between the power of the princes and the old freedom of the towns. A skilful exploitation of the

tensions between the common council of Berlin-Cölln and the
merchants of both towns allowed the elector Frederick II to make a
compromise which was highly favourable to the lord and his legal
position. An unsuccessful uprising in 1448 led to the complete subjection of the double town to the ruler's command. With the
unconditional and hard subjection of the proud town of Stendal,
the annihilation of the towns' privileges, the elimination of municipal coinage and court, the introduction of the ruler's control of the
council elections, the implementation of a ruthless taxation on the
part of the ruler, the independence of the Mark towns was essentially over. In the south, Nuremberg fought off the most talented,
but also the most brutal hater of the towns, the Franconian
Hohenzollern Albert Achilles and his noble followers, strongly and
with self-sacrifice in 1450, but suffered so terribly in subsequent
struggles, particularly through the ruthless plundering policies of
the 'fire-raising prince' Albert Alcibiades, that the town, though it
certainly survived this crisis with honour, was financially ruined.
But even then the town could write to the emperor: 'We have
only undergone these insuperable damages and spoliations because we did not wish to separate ourselves from your imperial
majesty, not to betray our duties'.

Thus in the same year of 1552 both Nuremberg and Strasbourg
(compare the beginning of our third chapter) were gravely dis-
appointed by the head of the empire. People have found fault with
the passivity of the towns in face of the attempts at imperial reform of the fifteenth century; but in doing so they have forgotten
that all these late medieval attempts at reform were being carried
out in favour of precisely that power whose victory the towns were
unable to encourage—that of the territorial princes. A definition
of the empire at the time of the proposed reform which would be
truer to the actual circumstances would be 'the firm under whose
aegis the princes pursued their common interests'. A glance at the
legal procedure suggested by the princes in 1437 is all that is
necessary to see why the towns had no choice but to oppose. Again
it is easy to say that the towns left each other in the lurch in emergencies, whereas the princes held together. But this judgment is
not generally valid. At the time when the princely territorial state

was becoming a reality the princes were much more in a position to agree upon military actions between themselves than were the towns they encircled; for them concerted action became less and less possible the more it was engaged in. The towns engaged in local particularism more or less against their will. There was nothing else they could do in a world of territorial states but form their own territories in order to keep the covetous neighbouring princes from their walls. The feeling of isolation, in an inimical world of increasing illegality and territorial princes caused this passivity to degenerate consecutively into gloomy discouragement and hopelessness.

The state-system which now imposed itself on the German towns was inadequate from the point of view of their foreign interests. Whereas in the Hansa, as far as the old customers and new competitors were concerned, the interests of the burghers were identified with those of the state, and the latter by virtue of this became furthermore a power which was indispensable to the individual towns, the German particularist state-system not only failed to give them the least bit of support but also consciously weakened the economic and political strength of individual towns. But what in the long run had a far worse effect on the German town was not the inadequacy of the German particularist state-system, but its incompatibility. The forces that were active within it were those of the victorious princes, of feudalism. For these states—large or diminutive—towns and townsmen were only to be thought of as objects to be ruled over, and not as sources of strength from which might be derived those forces in the state as a whole which would help to determine its outlook. We may compare the position of the English merchants within the English national state, their industrious participation in the Parliament, and we have a complete contrast. In the German separatist state there ruled the prince, and a nobility which was compensated for the loss of its independence with leading positions at the court, in the army and the government. The lawyer too played a leading part, frequently even the lawyer from the towns, although he thought of himself only as the servant of the prince and had forgotten his burgher origin as much as many an urban patrician had who had been elevated into the

40   Arms of the Empire and of the City of Nuremberg
From a design by Albrecht Dürer, 1521

country nobility. For all these reasons, and in complete contrast with other countries, integration into the state destroyed even the spiritual and intellectual foundations of the old merchant class in Germany. There began what for the history of Germany were the fateful centuries in which the class of the German population which in the Middle Ages had so splendidly stood the test even outside the country, the merchant upper class of the towns, was systematically weaned from political activity and thus politically ruined. Only now did the German town become small, dominated by parish-pump interests, and with the town and within the town the townsman became small, too. This was the sin the princely particularist state in Germany committed against the soul of the burgher—had to commit, on account of its miserable, mechanical and inorganic origins. Beneath the proud towers of Stendal at the time when it was a factor of importance in the great connections of the Hanseatic world, now lived a completely different race which no longer understood the testimonies to its own past. In place of the proud, upright bearing of a merchant class that had decided its own fate, and whose influence was widespread, there emerged the petty, spineless, submissive bearing of the subjects of later centuries. And thus was wasted one of the nation's best sources of strength—perhaps the best. From this point of view the work of a much later man, von Stein, only gains its full significance. From now on, in and between the territories, the German towns held on to a modest life, until the Thirty Years War annihilated what for most of them was still a not inconsiderable prosperity. Then, and only then, was formed what we call the common bourgeoisie with its characteristics of pettiness and spite—a form of life which characterises a late symptom of decline in the German burgher class, and not the class itself.

Certainly towards the end of the Middle Ages there were very serious tensions between the different sections of the population within the towns themselves, which numerous towns were not able to deal with by themselves. But in this connection we may note a high degree of political wisdom in the case of many towns whose leading classes made concessions, in conscious resignation, and knew how to arrive at a tolerable compromise between such violently opposed economic views as those represented by the workers and the merchants. Certain towns, such as Lübeck, managed to keep going for a surprisingly long time thanks to this resigned self-discipline. Only the creation of new possibilities setting great tasks to merchant enterprise could have brought real salvation—but this the German separatist states were unable to do. They were however created in the large national states, above all in England, and thus the blossoming of towns and the merchant class was transplanted from Germany to other lands. The German merchant lost that respected and revered position abroad which had evidently devolved upon him in the Middle Ages; his highly important political role outside Germany was played out. For from the moment when a central power was denied them the towns were defending a lost position. They had no choice, within a world of pseudo-states dissolving into little circles, but to form a small separatist state for themselves. This they did more or less successfully; the most successful perhaps was Nuremberg. Thus they became themselves supporters of the particularist idea, which was then expressed in a corresponding economic policy; thus they lost the high interest which until late in the Middle Ages they were entirely justified in laying claim to in the large-scale politics of Germany. At that time they had been the most eminent supporters of a political concept of the nation as a whole. Now the splendid spirit of the German towns, and the political abilities which had developed with it and through it, were smothered, and even transformed into their antithesis. In the world which was thrust upon the German towns from outside, and which was growing smaller and smaller, their road to greatness was lost.

BIBLIOGRAPHY

In the revised German edition of this book, there was a summary, critical bibliography, which included books published since the original appearance of Rörig's essay in the *Propyläen Weltgeschichte*. For the most part, these were books and articles written in German. Rörig was most concerned with German towns, and studies on German towns tend obviously to be written in German. There is, however, no point in reprinting such a bibliography, in a book intended particularly for those students who do not have enough German to read Rörig himself. The following select bibliography has been made with the principal object of enabling educated English students to follow up some of the themes in this book, as displayed in parts of Europe other than Germany. Where possible, books in English or French about German towns have been included, but it must be admitted that students of the German towns must expect to find most of the literature in German.

The German editor of Rörig's study pointed out that the work was conceived within certain limits. In the first place, the author limited himself in time and did not do more than generalise freely in the first chapter about the 'origins' of the towns; nor did he carry the history later than the early sixteenth century. Secondly the editor stressed that Rörig was not interested so much in the town, conceived as an urban area of greater or lesser size, but in the medieval town as a particular type of cultural and economic society, and consequently in the middle classes as a new element in medieval society and a determining factor in social history. This is why the book concentrates on the great leading towns in which this middle class was born and in which it developed the foundations of its legal and social autonomy, and on the medieval world which Rörig believed to be the necessary economic basis of the medieval town. This is why the names of the world cities of the time—Cologne, Strasbourg, Lübeck, Nuremberg, Regensburg and others in Germany, together with Venice, Florence, Genoa, Paris, Ghent, Bruges, Ypres, Antwerp and London—constantly reappear, for it was there that these developments took on their characteristic form. The book must not be misconceived as a detailed portrait of medieval towns. It is concerned with the function and structure of the town and the middle class, in as much as they had a vital bearing in their own day. It is in this sense that Rörig's *The Medieval Town* has attained the reputation of being a classical exposé.

GENERAL ECONOMIC BACKGROUND

There is a useful resumé by M. Mollat, P. Johansen, M. Postan, A. Sapori and C. Verlinden, 'L'économie européenne aux deux derniers siècles du moyen âge', in *Relazioni del X Congresso Internazionale di Scienze Storiche*, VI, 803–957, Florence, 1955. More recent is J. Heers, *L'occident aux XIVe et XVe siècles: aspects économiques et sociaux*, Paris, 1963. For England there is the stimulating book by A. R. Bridbury, *Economic Growth: England in the Later Middle Ages*, London, 1962. Other recommended general books are H. Pirenne, *Economic and Social History of Medieval Europe*, London 1936; F. C. Lane and J. C. Riemersma, *Enterprise and Secular Change*, London, 1953; C. M. Cipolla, *Money, Prices and Civilisation in the Mediterranean World*, Princeton, 1956; and A. Andreas, *Deutschland vor der Reformation: eine Zeitenwende*, 1932. There are also useful studies in the Cambridge Economic Histories: vol. I, *The Agrarian Life of the Middle Ages*, ed. M. Postan, 1966; vol. II, *Trade and Industry in the Middle Ages*, ed. M. Postan and E. E. Rich, 1952; vol. III, *Economic Organisation and Policies in the Middle Ages*, ed. M. Postan, E. E. Rich and E. Miller, 1963.

THE MEDIEVAL TOWN

The only works in English devoted entirely to the towns of medieval Europe are M. V. Clarke, *The Medieval City State*, London, 1926 (and recently reprinted) and the very summary book by J. H. Mundy and P. Riesenberg, *The Medieval Town*, New York, 1958. An earlier work of H. Pirenne was translated and published as *Medieval Cities*, Princeton, 1925. More general works on cities, which discuss the medieval periods are M. Weber, *The City*, London, 1960; R. E. Dickinson, *The West European City*, London, 1951 (2nd ed.) and L. Mumford, *The City in History*, London, 1961.

Invaluable as a work of reference is J. F. Niermeyer and C. Van de Kieft, *Elenchus fontium historiae urbanae: Recueils de textes d'histoire medievale*, 3 vols, Leiden, 1965. There is in English a recent study of very early medieval town-life, I. A. Argus, *Urban Civilisation in Pre-Crusade Europe*, Leiden, 1965. Notice also F. Ganshof, *Etude sur le dévelopment des villes d'entre Loire et Rhin au moyen âge*, Paris, 1943; R. Pernoud, *Les villes marchandes aux XIVe et XVe siècles*, Paris, 1948; L. Verriest, *Nouvelles Etudes d'histoire urbaine*, Gembloux, 1948 and G. Espinas, 'Histoire Urbaine, direction de recherches et résultats', in *Annales*, 1931, 394–427. Useful reviews of the latest work done into fields of urban history are to be found in the Recueils de la Société Jean Bodin, Brussels: vol. VI, *La Ville: Institutions Administratives et Judiciaires*, 1954; vol. VII, *La Ville: Institutions Economiques et Sociales*, 1955; vol. VIII, *La Ville: Le Droit Privé*, 1957. These are especially useful for the sections on Germany written in French. Of the many German works particularly recommended are E. Eunen, *Frühgeschichte der Europäischen Stadt*, Bonn, 1953 and Th. Meyer (ed.), *Studien zu den Anfängen des Europäischen Städtewesens*.

For the general problems of towns see M. Poète, *Introduction à l'urbanisme*, Paris, 1929; P. Lavedan, *Histoire de l'urbanisme;* vol. I, *Antiquité, Moyen Age;* vol. II, *Renaissance, Temps Modernes*, Paris, 1926–41; F. R. Hiorns, *Town-building in History*, London, 1956.

DEVELOPMENT OF TOWNS AND INSTITUTIONS

A. R. Lewis, 'Development of town government in twelfth-century Montpellier', *Speculum*, 1947, 51–67; R. Grand, 'La genèse du mouvement communal', *Revue de l'histoire du droit français et étranger*, 1940–41, vol. 20, n.s., 149–73; L. Chiappelli, 'La formazione storica del commune cittadino', *Archivo Storico Italiano*, 1926, vol. 2, 3–59; 1927, vol. 1, 177–229; 1928, vol. 2, 3–89; 1930, vol. 1, 3–59, vol. 2, 3–56.

R. Mounier, *Les institutions judiciaires des villes de Flandre des origines à la rédaction des coutumes*, Paris, 1924; Mounier, *Les institutions financières du comté de Flandre du XIe siècle à 1384*, Paris, 1948; J. Duesberg, *Les juridictions scabinales en Flandre et en Lotharingie au moyen âge*, Louvain, 1932; R. Byl, *Les juridictions scabinales dans le duché de Brabant des origines à la fin du XVe siècle*, Paris, 1965; M. Yans, *Pasicrisie des Echevins de Liège*, Liège, 1948–50. F. L. Ganshof, *Recherches sur les tribunaux du chatêllenie en Flandre*, Antwerp, 1932; G. Des Marez, *Etude sur la propriété foncière des villes au moyen âge*, Ghent, 1898; P. Godding, *Le droit foncier à Bruxelles au moyen âge*, Brussels, 1960; G. Espinas, *Les finances de la commune de Douai des origines au XVe siècle*, Paris, 1902; M. Moeder, *Les institutions de Mulhouse au moyen âge*, Paris, 1951. E. Pitz, *Die Entstehung der Ratsherrschaft in Nürnberg in 13 und 14 Jahrhundert*, Munich, 1956. R. Mols, *Introduction à la Démographie Historique des villes d'Europe du XIVe au XVIIIe siècles*, Louvain, 1954–56; J. C. Russell, *British Medieval Population*, Albuquerque, 1948. E. Carpenter, *Une ville devant la Peste: Orvieto et la Peste Noire de 1348*, Paris, 1962. C. Bücher, *Die Bevölkerung von Frankfurtam Main in XIV. und XV. Jahrhundert*, Tubingen, 1886.

ECONOMIC ACTIVITY OF THE TOWNS

R. Maunier, *L'origine et la fonction économique des villes*, Paris, 1910; C. Gross, *The Gild Merchant*, Oxford, 1890; G. Unwin, *The Guilds and Companies of London*, London, 1910; R. S. Smith, *The Spanish Guild Merchant*, 1250–1700, Durham N. C., 1940; E. Coornaert, *Les corporations en France avant 1789*, Paris, 1941; Coornaert, 'Les ghildes médiévales', *Revue Historique*, 1948 t. 199; E. Lousse, *La société d'ancien régime: organisation et représentation corporatives*, Louvain, 1943; E. Rodocanachi, *Les corporations ouvrières à Rome depuis la chute de Romain*, Paris, 1894; A. Doren, *Le Arti Florentine* (translated from the German), Florence, 1940; C. De Ribbe: *Les corporations ouvrières de l'ancien régime en Provence*, Aix, 1865; A.

Gouron: *La règlementation des métiers en Languedec au moyen âge*, Paris, 1958; M. Malowist, *Essai sur l'histoire du métier à l'époque de la crise de la féodalité en Europe occidentale aux XIVe et XVe siècles* (French summary), Warsaw, 1954. L. F. Salzman, *English Industries of the Middle Ages*, Oxford, 1923; G. Des Marez, *L'organisation du travail à Bruxelles au XVe siècle*, Brussels, 1904; G. Renard, *Histoire du travail à Florence*, Paris, 1913.

For the textile trades see E. Miller, 'The Fortunes of the English Textile Industry during the thirteenth century', *Economic History Review*, 1965, 64–82; G. Espinas, *La draperie dans la Flandre française au moyen âge*, Paris, 1923; H. van Werveke, 'Industrial Growth in the Middle Ages: the cloth industry in Flanders', *Economic History Review*, 1954, 237—45; R. de Roover, 'A Florentine firm of cloth manufacturers: management and organisation of a sixteenth-century business', *Speculum*, 1941, XVI, 3–33.

SOCIAL QUESTIONS

G. Le Bras, 'Les confréries chrétiennes', *Revue d'histoire du droit français et étranger*, t. XIX–XX, 1940–41, 4th series, 310–63; P. Wolff, 'Les Luttes sociales dans les villes du midi français XIIIe–XVe siècles', *Annales: Economies, sociétés, civilisations*, 1947, II, 443–54; Vörträge und Forschungen: *Die Gesellschaftliche Struktur der mittelalterlichen Städte in Europa*, Konstanz, 1966; J. Schildhauer, *Soziale politische und religiöse Auseinandersetzung in den Hanse städten Stralsund, Rostock und Weimar im ersten drittel des 16 Jahrhunderts*, Weimar, 1959; J. W. Parkes, *The Jew in the Medieval Community, a Study of his Political and Economic Situation*, London, 1938; G. Kisch, *The Jews in Medieval Germany*, Chicago, 1949; J. Stengers, *Les juifs dans les Pays-Bas au moyen âge*, Brussels, 1950; J. M. Vincent, *Costume and Conduct in the Laws of Basel, Bern and Zürich*, Baltimore, 1935; N. Newett, 'The Sumptuary Laws of Venice in the Fourteenth and Fifteenth Centuries', *Historical Essays by members of Owens College, Manchester*, ed. T. F. Tout and J. Tait, London, 1920.

BUSINESS AFFAIRS

G. Espinas, *Les origines du capitalisme*, 4 vols. Lille, 1933–49. M. Beard, *A History of the Business Man*, New York, 1938; F. Edler, *Glossary of Medieval Terms of Business: Italian Series 1200–1600*,

Cambridge (Mass.) 1934; F. Balducci Pegolotti, *La pratica della mercatura*, ed. A. Evans, Cambridge (Mass.) 1936; R. J. Reynolds, 'Origins of Modern Business Enterprise', *Journal of Economic History* 1952, vol. XII, 350–65; E. E. Hirschler 'Medieval Economic Competition', *Journal of Economic History*, 1954, vol. XIV, 52–8; A. P. Usher, *The early history of deposit banking in Mediterranean Europe*, Cambridge (Mass.), 1943; R. de Roover, *Money, Banking and Credit in Medieval Bruges*, Cambridge (Mass.), 1948; Roover, *The Rise and Decline of the Medici Bank*, Cambridge (Mass.), 1963; Roover, *L'évolution de la lettre de change XIVe–XVIIIe siècles*, Paris 1953; Roover, 'The development of accounting prior to Luca Pacioli, according to the account books of medieval merchants', *Studies in the History of Accounting*, ed. A. C. Littleton and B. S. Yamey, London, 1956; Roover, 'The Story of the Alberti Company 1302–48, as revealed in its account books', *Business History Review*, 1958, XXXII, 14–59; J. C. Ayats, F. Udine and S. Alemany, *La taula de cambio de Barcelona, 1416–1714*, Barcelona, 1947; A. E. Sayous 'La technique des affaires; un contrat de société à Barcelone: la table des échanges de Valence', *Annales d'histoire économique et sociale*, 1934, année VI, 133–7; J. Craig, *The Mint: a History of the London Mint from A.D. 287 to 1948*, Cambridge, 1953; H. Laurent, *La loi de Gresham au moyen âge: Essai sur la circulation monétaire entre la Flandre et le Brabant à la fin du XIVe siècle*, Paris, 1938; H. van Werveke, 'Currency Manipulation in the Middle Ages: the Case of Louis de Mâle, Count of Flanders', *Transactions of the Royal Historical Society*, 4th series 1949, vol. XXXI 115–27; A. Grundzweig, 'Les incidences internationales des mutations monétaires de Philippe le Bel', *Moyen Age*, 1953, LIX, 117–72; C. M. Cipolla, 'Currency depreciation in medieval Europe', *Economic History Review*, 1962, 413–21; J. W. Baldwin, *Medieval Theories of the Just Price*, Philadelphia, 1959; R. de Roover, 'The Concept of the Just Price Theory of Economic Policy', *Journal of Economic History*, 1959, vol. XVIII, 418–34; B. N. Nelson, *The idea of usury*, Princeton, 1949; J. T. Noonan, *The Scholastic Analysis of Usury*, Cambridge (Mass.), 1957; T. D. McLaughlin 'The Teachings of the Canonists on Usury', *Medieval Studies*, 1939, I, 81–147; 1940, II, 1–22; F. C. Lane, 'Tonnages Medieval and Modern', *Economic History Review*, 1964; F. Valls i Taberner, *Consulat de Mar*, Barcelona,

1930; E. H. Byrne, *Genoese Shipping in the twelfth and thirteenth centuries*, Cambridge (Mass.), 1930; F. C. Lane, *Venetian Ships and Shipbuilding of the Renaissance*, Baltimore, 1934; C. M. Cipolla, *Guns and Sails in the early phase of European expansion 1400–1700*, London, 1965.

HISTORIES OF TRADE

M. Mollat (ed.) *Les sources de l'histoire maritime en Europe du moyen âge au XVIIIe siècle*, Paris, 1962; J. Lacour-Gayet, *Histoire du commerce*, vol. I, part ii, by M. Boulet, 'Le Moyen Age', Paris, 1950; W. von Heyd, *Histoire du commerce du Levant au moyen âge* (French translation), Leipzig, 1885–86; R. S. Lopez and I. W. Raymond, *Medieval Trade in the Mediterranean World*, New York, 1955; L. Olschki, *Marco Polo's Predecessors*, Baltimore, 1943; C. Cahen *Douanes et commerce dans les ports méditerranéens de l'Egypt mediévale*, Leiden, 1965; L. F. Salzman, *English Trade in the Middle Ages*, Oxford, 1931; N. S. B. Gras, *The Early English Customs System*, Cambridge, (Mass.), 1918; E. M. Carus-Wilson and O. Coleman, *England's Export Trade 1275–1547*, Oxford, 1963; G. Unwin, *Finance and Trade under Edward III*, Manchester, 1918; E. Power and M. Postan, *Studies in English Trade in the Fifteenth Century*, 2nd ed., 1951; E. Power, *The Wool Trade in English Medieval History*, Oxford, 1941; A. R. Bridbury, *England and the Salt Trade in the Later Middle Ages*, Oxford, 1955, E. M. Veale: *The English Fur Trade in the Later Middle Ages*, Oxford, 1966; N. S. B. Gras, *The Evolution of the English Corn Market*, Cambridge (Mass.), 1906; H. Laurent, *Un grand commerce d'exportation au moyen age: la draperie du Pays-Bas en France et dans les pays méditerranéens XIIe–XIVe siècles*, Paris, 1935; J. Craeybeckx, *Un grand commerce d'importation: les vins de France aux anciens Pays-Bas XIIe–XVIe siècles*, Paris, 1958; Y. Renouard, 'Le grand commerce des vins de Gascogne au moyen age', *Revue Historique*, CCXXI, 1959, 261–304; R. Doerhaerd, *Les relations commerciales entre Gênes, la Belgique et l'Outremont d'après les archives notariales génoises aux XIIe et XIVe siècles*, Brussels, 1941; N. J. M. Kerling; *Commercial Relations of Holland and Zeeland with England from the Late Thirteenth Century to the Close of the Middle Ages*, Leiden, 1954; M. Mollat, *Le commerce maritime normand à la fin du moyen âge*, Paris, 1952; G. Rambert (ed.)

Histoire du commerce de Marseille, Marseille, 1949; H. van Werveke, *Bruges et Anvers: Huit siècles de commerce flamand*, Brussels, 1944; A. Schulte, *Geschichte der Grossen Ravensburger Handels gesellschaft 1380–1530*, 3 vols, Stuttgart 1923.

ENGLISH TOWNS

J. Tait, *The Medieval English Borough*, Manchester, 1936; C. Stephenson, *Borough and Town*, Cambridge (Mass.), 1933; C. R. Young, *The English Borough and Royal Administration 1130–1307*, Durham N.C., 1961; G. A. Williams, *Medieval London: From Commune to Capital*, London, 1963; S. Thrupp, *The Merchant Class of Medieval London 1300–1500*, Chicago, 1948; M. K. James, 'A London Merchant of the Fourteenth Century', *Economic History Review*, 1956, VIII, 364–76; J. W. F. Hill, *Medieval Lincoln*, Cambridge 1948; A. A. Ruddock, *Italian Merchants and Shipping in Southampton 1270–1600*, Southampton, 1951; O. Coleman, 'Trade and Prosperity in the Fifteenth Century: Some Aspects of the Trade of Southampton, *Economic History Review*, 1963, 9–22; E. Carus-Wilson, *Medieval Merchant Venturers*, London, 1954; A. Beardwood, *Alien Merchants in England 1350–77*, Cambridge (Mass.), 1931; G. A. Holmes, 'Florentine Merchants in England 1346–1436', *Economic History Review*, XIII, 1960, 193–208; M. Mallet, 'Anglo-Florentine Commercial Relations 1465–92', *Economic History Review*, 1962, 250–65.

FRENCH TOWNS

C. Petit-Dutaillis, *Les Communes françaises*, Paris, 1947; P. A. Chéruel, *Histoire de Rouen pendant l'époque communal 1150–1382*, Rouen, 1843–44: L. Halphen, *Paris sous les premiers Capétiens (987–1223)*, Paris, 1909; G. Espinas, *La vie urbaine de Douai au moyen âge*, Paris, 1913; Espinas, *Une guerre sociale interurbaine dans la Flandre wallone au XIIIe siècle: Douai et Lille 1284–85*, Paris 1930; N. Denholm-Young, 'The Merchants of Cahors', *Medievalia et Humanistica*, 1946; G. Lesage, *Marseille Angevine: recherches sur son évolution administrative économique et urbaine 1264–1348*, Paris, 1950; P. Wolff, *Commerces et marchands à Toulouse vers 1350-vers 1450*, Paris, 1954; J. B. Wadsworth *Lyons 1473–1503*, Cambridge (Mass.), 1962.

SPANISH AND PORTUGUESE TOWNS

J. Klein, *The Mesta, a Study in Spanish Economic History*, Cambridge (Mass.) 1920; J. Vicens-Vives, *Férran II i la ciutat de Barcelona 1479–1516*, Barcelona, 1936; A. de Oliveira Marques, *Hansa e Portugal na Idade Média*, Lisbon, 1959.

ITALIAN TOWNS

G. Luzzatto, *An Economic History of Italy from the Fall of the Roman Empire to the Beginning of the Sixteenth Century* (translation by P. Jones), London, 1961; C. M. Cipolla, 'The Trends in Italian Economic History in the Later Middle Ages', *Economic History Review*, 1949, 181–4; D. Waley, *Medieval Orvieto*, Cambridge, 1952; D. Herlihy, *Pisa in the Early Renaissance, a Study of Urban Growth*, New Haven, 1958; J. K. Hyde, *Padua in the age of Dante*, Manchester, 1966; F. Schevill, *History of Florence*, London, 1937; G. A. Brucker, *Florentine Politics and Society*, Princeton, 1962; F. C. Lane, *Venice and History*, Lane, *Andrea Barbarigo, Merchant of Venice 1418–39*, Baltimore, 1944; J. Heers, *Gênes au XVe siècle, activité économique et problemes sociaux*, Paris, 1961; P. Jones, 'Communes and Despots: the City State in Late Medieval Italy', *Transactions of the Royal Historical Society*, 5th series vol. xv, 1965, 71–96; A. Sapori, *Le marchand italien au moyen âge*, Paris, 1952; Y. Renouard, *Les Hommes d'affaires italiens du moyen âge*, Paris, 1949; Renouard, *Les relations des papes d'Avignon et des compagnies commerciales et bancaires de 1316 à 1378*, Paris, 1941; I. Origo, *Merchant of Prato, Francesco di Marco Datini 1335–1410*, London, 1957; D. F. Dowd, 'The Economic Exapansion of Lombardy 1300–1500, a Study in Political Stimulus to Economic Change', *Journal of Economic History* 1961, XXI, 143–60.

FLEMISH TOWNS

J. Lestocquoy, *Les villes de Flandre et d'Italie sous le gouvernement des patriciens XIe–XVe siècles*, Paris, 1952; H. Pirenne, *Belgian Democracy*, Manchester, 1904; Pirenne, *Histoire de Belgique*, 5th ed., Brussels, 1929–32; Pirenne, *Les villes et les institutions urbaines*, Brussels, 1939; E. Coornaerts, *Les français et le commerce international à Anvers, fin du XVe–XVIe siècles*, Paris, 1961; H. van der Wee, *The Growth of the Antwerp market in the European Economy*, The Hague, 1963; H. van

Werveke, *Gand: Esquisse d'histoire sociale*, Brussels, 1946; G. Kurth, *La Cité de Liège au moyen âge*, Liège, 1909; F. Vercauteren, *Luttes sociales à Liège aux XIIIe et XIVe siècles*, Brussels, 1943; J. Lejeune, *Liège et son Pays: Naissance d'une patrie (XIIIe–XIVe siècles)*, Liège, 1948; C. J. Joset, *Les Villes au pays de Luxembourg 1196–1383*, Louvain, 1940; R. Feenstra, *Les Villes des Pay Bas septentrionaux: Histoire des institutions administratives et judiciaires*.

GERMAN AND BALTIC TOWNS

P. Dollinger, *La Hanse (XIIe–XVIIe siècles)*, Paris, 1964; F. L. Carsten, *The Origins of Prussia*, Oxford, 1954; J. A. Gade, *The Hanseatic Control of Norwegian Commerce during the Late Middle Ages*, Leiden, 1951; F. Rörig, 'Les raisons intellectuelles d'une suprematie commerciale: La Hanse', *Annales d'histoire économique et Sociale*, 1930, I, 481–94; M. Malowist, 'The Economic and Social Development of the Baltic Countries from the Fifteenth to the Seventeeth Centuries', *Economic History Review*, 1959, 177–89; P. Sawyer, *The Age of the Vikings*, London, 1962; L. Musset, *Les peuples scandinaves au moyen âge*, Paris, 1961; J. Schneider, *La ville de Metz aux XIIIe et XIVe siècles*, Paris, 1950; P. E. Martin, *Histoire de Genève des origines à 1798*, Geneva, 1951; M. Planitz, *Die Deutsche Stadt in Mittelalter*, Cologne, 1954; R. Koetzsche und W. Ebert, *Geschichte der osdeutschen Kolonisation*, Leipzig, 1937; E. Keyser, *Deutsches Städtebuch Handbuch Städtischer Geschichte*, 4 volumes so far published 1939–62; Keyser, *Städtegründungen ünd Städtebau in Nordwestdeutschland im Mittelalter*, Remagen, 1959; *Städtewesen und Bürgertum als geschichtliche Kräfte, Gedächtnisschrift für F. Rörig*, ed. A. von Brandt und W. Koppe, Lübeck, 1953; A. von Brandt, *Geist und Politik in der Lübeckischen Geschichte*, Lübeck, 1954; H. Reincke, *Forschungen und Skizzen zur hamburgischen Geschichte*, Hamburg, 1951; H. Vogts, *Köln im Spiegel seiner Kunst*, Cologne, 1950; H. Planitz und T. Buyken (ed.) *Die Kölner Schreinsbücher der 13 und 14 Jahrhunderts*, Weimar, 1937; E. Lauer, 'The South German Reichstädte in the Later Middle Ages', *Medieval and Historiographical Essays in honour of James Westfall Thompson*, Chicago, 1938; L. Schick, *Un grand homme d'affaires au début du XVIe siècle: Jacob Fugger*, Paris, 1957.

INDEX

❀

The numerals in **bold type** refer to the figure number of the illustrations